CONTEMPORARY CRITICAL CRIMINOLOGY

The concept of critical criminology – that crime and the present-day processes of criminalization are rooted in the core structures of society – is of more relevance today than it has been at any other time.

Written by an internationally renowned scholar, *Contemporary Critical Criminology* introduces the most up-to-date empirical, theoretical, and political contributions made by critical criminologists around the world. In its exploration of this material, the book also challenges the erroneous but widely held notion that the critical criminological project is restricted to mechanically applying theories to substantive topics, or to simply calling for radical political, economic, cultural, and social transformations.

This book is an essential source of reference for both undergraduate and postgraduate students of Criminology, Criminal Theory, Social Policy, Research Methodology, and Penology.

Walter S. DeKeseredy is Professor of Criminology, Justice and Policy Studies at the Ontario University Institute of Technology, Canada. He is the author or co-author of 13 books on topics such as abuse of women, crime and poverty in public housing, and women in conflict with the law, and has also written over 70 scientific journal articles. Dr. DeKeseredy has received awards for his research from the American Society of Criminology's Division on Critical Criminology and Division on Women and Crime, as well as the Linda Saltzman Memorial Intimate Violence Researcher Award from the Institute on Violence, Abuse and Trauma.

KEY IDEAS IN CRIMINOLOGY

SERIES EDITOR: TIM NEWBURN is Professor of Criminology and Social Policy, Director of the Mannheim Centre for Criminology, London School of Economics and President of the British Society of Criminology. He has written and researched widely on issues of crime and justice.

Key Ideas in Criminology explores the major concepts, issues, debates, and controversies in criminology. The series aims to provide authoritative essays on central topics within the broader area of criminology. Each book adopts a strong individual "line," constituting original essays rather than literature surveys, and offers lively and agenda-setting treatments of their subject matter.

These books will appeal to students, teachers, and researchers in criminology, sociology, social policy, cultural studies, law, and political science.

CONTEMPORARY CRITICAL CRIMINOLOGY

Walter S. DeKeseredy

LONDON AND NEW YORK

First published 2011
by Routledge
2 Park Square, Milton Park, Abingdon, Oxon OX14 4RN

Simultaneously published in the USA and Canada
by Routledge
711 Third Avenue, New York, NY 10017, USA

Routledge is an imprint of the Taylor & Francis Group, an informa business

© 2011 Walter S. DeKeseredy

Typeset in Sabon by Wearset Ltd, Boldon, Tyne and Wear

British Library Cataloguing in Publication Data
A catalogue record for this book is available from the British Library

Library of Congress Cataloging-in-Publication Data
DeKeseredy, Walter S., 1959–
Contemporary critical criminology/by Walter S.
DeKeseredy.
p. cm.
Includes bibliographical references.
1. Critical criminology. 2. Criminology. I. Title.
HV6019.D45 2010
364–dc22   2010004664

ISBN13: 978-0-415-55667-5 (hbk)
ISBN13: 978-0-415-55666-8 (pbk)
ISBN13: 978-0-203-86923-9 (ebk)

Contents

PREFACE

In June of 1986, I would have never dreamed of writing this book. I was a second-year Ph.D. student with a keen interest in critical criminology, and I presented a paper titled "Marxist Criminology in Canada: Toward Linking Theory with Practice" at the Canadian Sociology and Anthropology conference in Winnipeg, Canada. I did not have a sophisticated understanding of critical criminology and thus did not expect my paper to be well received. However, things went worse than I anticipated. The discussant on my panel was a pioneer in the field and he sharply criticized my work in front of an audience of seasoned scholars for nearly 30 minutes. My self-esteem was shattered and I thought my career was over. I also vowed never to engage with critical criminology again. As is often said, "Never say never."

My supervisory committee helped me move forward and continue working on my dissertation. So, eager to keep up with new developments in my area of research, I attended the American Society of Criminology conference in Atlanta in November 1986 and went to sessions featuring prominent critical criminologists such as Meda Chesney-Lind, Kathleen Daly, Susan Caringella, Dorie Klein, Betsy Stanko, Russell and Rebecca Dobash, and Claire Renzetti. I was deeply moved by their passion, research, and critiques of mainstream research, theories, and policies. Their voices also started to rekindle my interest in critical criminology and they offered me alternative ways of understanding the social world.

Although these and other progressive scholars' presentations were in and of themselves important to me, what also brought me back to critical criminology was a long conversation I had with Kathleen Daly, Meda Chesney-Lind, Dorie Klein, and Betsy Stanko in a bar located in the conference hotel. They inspired me to pursue my inner desire to engage in feminist inquiry and other ways of thinking critically about crime. I would not be doing what I am doing today without their kindness, collegiality, and compassion. My dear friend and colleague Martin Schwartz also played a key role in returning me to critical criminology. I met Marty in 1987 and we have worked very closely together ever since.

There are actually quite a few good books on critical criminology, which is one of the key reasons I was somewhat reluctant to write this one. However, Routledge editor Gerhard Boomgaarden enthusiastically encouraged me to contribute a book on the topic to the *Key Ideas in Criminology* series edited by Tim Newburn. I am grateful for their support and hope that my project adds to the rapidly growing international body of critical criminological scholarship. Indeed, as I learned from working on this book, keeping up with the extant literature in the field constitutes a major ongoing challenge.

Contemporary Critical Criminology has several main objectives, one of which is to review my colleagues' recent empirical, theoretical, and political contributions. Another goal is to show that, contrary to what many conservative scholars claim, critical criminologists are heavily involved in theory construction and theory testing, and use a variety of research methods to gather qualitative and quantitative data. Critical criminologists also don't simply call for radical social, political, and economic change. Although this is one of their central goals, progressive scholars and activists also propose numerous short-term ways of chipping away at broader social forces that influence crime and buttress unjust laws and methods of social control. Hence, recent examples of such initiatives are discussed.

Chapter 1 offers readers a brief history and definition of critical criminology. Of course, an unknown number of readers will disagree with my historical account. Still, as Raymond Michalowski states in his 1996 story of critical criminology: "This is all to the good. I increasingly suspect that we can best arrive at useful truth by telling and hearing multiple versions of the same story" (Michalowski, 1996, p. 9).

Chapter 2 demonstrates that critical criminology has gone through a number of significant theoretical changes since its birth in the early 1970s. Special attention is paid to briefly reviewing and evaluating major new directions, such as cultural criminology, convict criminology, feminist theories, and recent variants of left realist thought. Undoubtedly, new perspectives will be offered by the time you finish reading this book.

Critical criminologists have done much empirical work over the past 40 years, and a key objective of Chapter 3 is to show that critical criminology is much more than a theoretical and/or political enterprise. Examples of recent research are presented, but the studies reviewed are not considered better than those not examined. Obviously, it is impossible to review all critical criminological empirical projects in one chapter or book.

What is to be done about crime, law, and social control? Chapter 4 shows that just because critical scholars call for major political, economic, social, and cultural transformations does not mean that they disregard short-term reforms. However, rather than repeat what has been said in previous critical texts, this chapter presents some new initiatives, such as using computer technology to protest government policies. It is necessary to create policies and practices that meet the unique needs of people in an ever-changing world, and the Internet is an effective means of facilitating social change.

Critical criminology is often criticized for being "gender-blind." True, early works, such as Taylor, Walton, and Young's (1973) *The New Criminology*, said nothing about women and the gendered nature of society; however, things have changed considerably since the publication of this seminal book. Thus, materials on women and gender are integrated into every chapter at relevant points. It isn't only gender issues that are fully integrated; race, class, *and* gender are treated as equally important and are brought up whenever they are relevant. Nevertheless, the bulk of the material on these factors are recent contributions, which is why this book is titled *Contemporary Critical Criminology*.

ACKNOWLEDGMENTS

This book is the product of a collective effort. Again, it would not have been written without Gerhard Boomgaarden's kind invitation and support. Gerhard deeply cares about his authors and I count myself lucky to have had the pleasure of working closely with him. Series editor Tim Newburn also played a key role in bringing this book to fruition and I greatly respect his scholarly rigor and many important contributions to a social scientific understanding of some of the world's most compelling social problems. Routledge editorial assistant Jennifer Dodd became involved in this project shortly before it was completed and her patience and encouragement will always be remembered.

Others also deserve special recognition. Joseph F. Donnermeyer, David O. Friedrichs, Christopher W. Mullins, Stephen L. Muzzatti, Dawn Rothe, Martin D. Schwartz, and Phillip Shon took time away from their very busy schedules to carefully read drafts of each chapter despite having many responsibilities (including writing their own books, articles, etc.). I am thankful for their friendship, and they are scholars in the true spirit of the word. Their comments made this book better than it otherwise would have been.

Over the years I have greatly benefited from the comments, criticisms, lessons, emotional support, and influences of these progressive friends and colleagues: Bernie Auchter, Karen Bachar, Gregg Barak, Raquel Kennedy Bergen, Helene Berman, Henry Brownstein, Susan Caringella, Meda Chesney-Lind, Taylor Churchill, Kimberly J. Cook, Francis T. Cullen, Elliott Currie, Kathleen Daly, Molly Dragiewicz, Desmond Ellis, Jeff Ferrell, Bonnie Fisher, Alberto Godenzi, Judith Grant, Ronald Hinch, David Kauzlarich, Dorie Klein, Julian Lo, Michael J. Lynch, Brian D. MacLean, James W. Messerschmidt, Raymond

J. Michalowski, Jody Miller, Susan L. Miller, Dragan Milovanovic, Louise Moyer, Patrik Olsson, Barbara Owen, Ruth Peterson, Mike Presdee, Lori Post, Claire M. Renzetti, Robin Robinson, Jeffrey Ian Ross, Aysan Sev'er, Susan Sharp, the late Michael D. Smith, Cris Sullivan, Betsy Stanko, Kenneth D. Tunnell, and Jock Young. Because many of these people disagree with one another, I assume full responsibility for the material presented in this book.

Contemporary Critical Criminology could not have been completed without the ongoing support of Pat and Andrea DeKeseredy and Eva Jantz. My "fur children" Captain, Drew, Mr. Higgins, Ola B. (named after feminist psychologist Ola Barnett), and Phoebe were also sources of much support. They constantly remind me that critical criminologists need to think about the roles played by cats and dogs in the day-to-day struggle to eliminate all forms of inequality.

This book includes material adapted from Walter S. DeKeseredy, "Review of Elliott Currie's *The Road to Whatever: Middle-Class Culture and the Crisis of Adolescence,*" *Critical Criminology* (2007); Walter S. DeKeseredy, "Canadian Crime Control in the New Millennium: The Influence of Neo-Conservative U.S. Policies and Practices," *Police Practice and Research: An International Journal* (2009a); Walter S. DeKeseredy, *Violence Against Women in Canada* (in press a); Walter S. DeKeseredy, Shahid Alvi, and Martin D. Schwartz, "Left Realism Revisited," in Walter S. DeKeseredy and Barbara Perry (Eds), *Advancing Critical Criminology* (2006); Walter S. DeKeseredy, Shahid Alvi, and Desmond Ellis, *Deviance and Crime: Theory, Research and Policy* (2005); Walter S. DeKeseredy and Patrik Olsson, "Adult Pornography, Male Peer Support, and Violence Against Women: The Contribution of the 'Dark Side' of the Internet," in M. Varga Martin and M.A. Garcia-Ruiz (Eds), *Technology for Facilitating Humanity and Combating Social Deviations: Interdisciplinary Perspectives* (in press); Walter S. DeKeseredy and Barbara Perry, "Introduction to Part I," in Walter S. DeKeseredy and Barbara Perry (Eds), *Advancing Critical Criminology* (2006); Walter S. DeKeseredy and Martin D. Schwartz, "British and U.S. Left Realism: A Critical Comparison," *International Journal of Offender Therapy and*

Comparative Criminology (1991); Walter S. DeKeseredy and Martin D. Schwartz, *Contemporary Criminology* (1996); Walter S. DeKeseredy and Martin D. Schwartz, *Woman Abuse on Campus: Results from the Canadian National Survey* (1998); and Walter S. DeKeseredy and Martin D. Schwartz, "Friedman Economic Policies, Social Exclusion and Crime: Toward a Gendered Left Realist Subcultural Theory," *Crime, Law and Social Change* (in press).

1

CRITICAL CRIMINOLOGY

DEFINITION AND BRIEF HISTORY

> [P]ossessive individualism is crumbling under its own weight of numbers. Despite building more and more prisons, despite incarcerating or seeking to control (by electronic or social engineering) human activity, the centre does not hold, mere anarchy holds sway. For at the heart of society there remains the "genetic" code of private property. It is inconceivable that criminology wedded to the "cure" rather than the causes of crime can in any way help permanently to resolve the crime problem. This would be the medical equivalent of accepting that an expanding tobacco industry and growing cancers are inevitable.
>
> (Walton, 1998, p. 3)

In the current era, much, if not all, of the world was (and probably still is) experiencing numerous economic, social, and political crises. For example, 400,000 jobs were lost in Canada since the fall of 2008, and in September 2009 Diane Finley, federal Human Resources Minister, argued strongly against cutting the minimum work requirements to qualify for employment insurance (Whittington, 2009a).[1] The summer of 2009 was, to say the least, also depressing for many Canadian youths aged 18–24. Approximately one out of every four Canadians in this age group was unemployed; with a sizeable portion unable to pay university or college tuition in the fall (Galt, 2009). Simultaneously, the youth unemployment rate in the United States hit a record high of 18.5 percent (Bureau of Labor Statistics, 2009).

The North American unemployment situation is not likely to improve in the near future. As Canadian Parliamentary Budget Officer Kevin Page noted in July 2009, Canada could lose 1.2 million jobs in 2009 and 2010. He also predicted that the federal budget deficit over five years will reach C$155.9 billion (Whittington, 2009b). With such high rates of unemployment comes chronic poverty, which in turn spawns more predatory violent street crimes, illegal drug use and dealing, and a myriad of other injurious symptoms of "turbo-charged capitalism" in poor communities (DeKeseredy, Alvi, Schwartz, and Tomaszewski, 2003; Luttwak, 1995).

As paid work in advanced capitalist countries and elsewhere rapidly disappears, we still witness many highly injurious effects of patriarchal gender relations. For instance, the World Health Organization conducted a multi-country study of the health effects of domestic violence. Over 24,000 women who resided in urban and rural parts of 10 countries were interviewed: the research team discovered that the percentage of women who were ever physically or sexually assaulted (or both) by an intimate partner ranged from 15 percent to 71 percent, with most research sites ranging between 29 percent and 62 percent (Garcia-Moreno, Jansen, Ellsberg, Heise, and Watts, 2005).

Another major international study – the International Violence Against Women Survey (IVAWS) – conducted interviews with 23,000 women in 11 countries. The percentage of women who revealed at least one incident of physical or sexual violence by any man since the age of 16 ranged from 20 percent in Hong Kong to between 50 percent and 60 percent in Australia, Costa Rica, the Czech Republic, Denmark, and Mozambique. In most countries examined, rates of victimization were above 35 percent (Johnson, Ollus, and Nevala, 2008). Consider, too, that in Australia, Canada, Israel, South Africa, and the United States, 40–70 percent of female homicide victims were murdered by their current or former partners (DeKeseredy, in press a; Krug, Dahlberg, and Mercy et al., 2002). Another frightening fact is that 14 girls and women are killed each day in Mexico (Mujica and Ayala, 2008). Of course, male violence against female intimates takes many other shapes and forms, such as honor killings, dowry-related violence, and acid burning (Sev'er, 2008; Silvestri and Crowther-Dowey, 2008; Watts and Zimmerman, 2002). Annually, approximately 5,000 women and girls lose their lives to honor killings around the world (Proudfoot, 2009).

Racism, in its many shapes and forms, is also very much alive and well throughout the world despite major legislative changes and the ongoing efforts of human-rights groups and activists. In the United States, for example, 23 percent of Native Americans live below the poverty line, compared to 12 percent of the general population. To make matters worse, the poverty rate on US Native reservations is over 50 percent (Housing Assistance Council, 2002; Perry, 2009a). And, as Turpin-Petrosino (2009, p. 21) reminds us, in the United States, "[s]ome of the most notorious hate crimes ever committed have targeted blacks." Black US males are also incarcerated at a per capita rate six times higher than their white counterparts. Further, about 11 percent of black men aged 30–34 are incarcerated (Human Rights Watch, 2008).

What is to be done about unemployment, violence against women, racism, and a host of other problems that plague countries characterized by structured social inequality? Guided by the views of the late University of Chicago economist Milton Friedman (1962),[2] many people on the right, like former US President George W. Bush, contend that the solutions to the world's problems are found in the following trinity: the elimination of the public sector; total corporate liberation; and skeletal social spending (N. Klein, 2007). Ironically, many conservatives do not seem to have a problem spending taxpayers' money on building more prisons and incarcerating more people. For example, California is home to the largest prison system in the United States, and this state's corrections budget was $2.1 billion annually at the end of the 1980s. In 2008–2009, California's corrections budget rose to $10.1 billion (Legislative Analyst's Office, 2010).

Correction facilities now constitute a major industry in the United States and United Kingdom. There is a rapid growth in private prisons and many stock analysts are encouraging their clients to invest in major companies operating facilities such as the GEO Group, formally known as Wackenhut Securities (Reiman and Leighton, 2010). Private companies claim to run prisons at 10–20 percent lower cost than US state governments, but Austin and Coventry's (2001) study – sponsored by the National Institute of Justice – found it was only 1 percent.

If there is a military–industrial complex that profits from the wars in Iraq and Afghanistan, there is also a "prison–industrial complex" that gains from crime at the taxpayers' expense (Schlosser, 1998). Thus, it is more than fair to assume that big business has a vested interest in ensuring that crime rates stay high and that the incarceration rate – like profits – constantly grows (Selman and Leighton, 2010). As Reiman and Leighton (2010) note:

> [T]he rich get richer BECAUSE the poor get prison! Consider that in 2007, the top wage earner at CCA made $2.8 million and his counterpart at the Geo Group made $3.8 million, including stock options and all bonuses; the annual retainer for serving on the Board of Directors of either company is $50,000 (plus several thousand dollars for each meeting that Board members attend), which is close to the median household income of the United States in 2007.
>
> (p. 177; emphasis in original)

Not all conservatives view prisons or other elements of the criminal justice system as the primary cures for crime. One recent example is Canadian psychologist Donald Dutton (2006), who prefers "treating" wife-beaters to mandatory arrest policies. Like prisons, psychotherapy, counseling, psychosurgery, or any of a number of other techniques designed to help offenders identify and deal with their problems contribute little, if anything, to lowering crime rates. Such strategies suffer from what Elliott Currie (1985) calls the "fallacy of autonomy." The idea of autonomy is that people act on their own, without the influence of others. The implication of theories that inform individual treatment is that peer groups and broader social forces have little impact on people's behaviors, attitudes, norms, and values (DeKeseredy and Schwartz, 1996). Those who break the law are seen as living in a "world strangely devoid of social or economic consequences, even of history" (Currie, 1985, p. 215).

This is true of some offenders. However, most violent street crimes, especially those committed by youths, are committed in groups (Warr, 2002). This is why incarcerating or "treating" several gang members does nothing to lower the rate of violent crime in the United States (Currie, 2008a). You can lock people up or make them undergo therapy, but such measures do not eliminate the social, psychological, or interpersonal forces that influence people to harm others. For every gang member you take off the street, others will replace him or her.

If people's peers motivate them to commit violent acts, the same can be said about broader structural forces. It is, for example, not surprising that the violent crime rate in the United States is higher than that of most other highly industrialized societies (Currie, 2008a; Van Dijk, 2008). It is well known that the United States is a nation characterized by gross economic inequality, poverty, high infant mortality rates, homelessness, and inadequate social support services (for example, unemployment insurance and health care) (Schwartz and DeKeseredy, 2008). High rates of violent acts are major symptoms of these problems (DeKeseredy *et al.*, 2003), and these crimes are committed mainly by groups of "underclass" people, sometimes referred to as "the truly disadvantaged" (Blau and Blau, 1982; Wilson, 1987). In fact, social and economic inequality – not personality or biological factors – are the most powerful predictors of most violent crimes (DeKeseredy, in press a).

Are there useful and meaningful alternatives to conventional wisdom about crime and its control? In other words, is there a progressive school of thought that sees crime as something other than a property of the individual and that views broader social, political, and economic change as the best solution to crimes in the streets, suites, and domestic/intimate settings? Anyone familiar with social scientific empirical, theoretical, and policy work would quickly point out that sociologists provide different ways of thinking about crime, deviance, and social control. Indeed, they do and some of them have had an important impact on public policy over the past 50 years. Consider strain theorists Richard Cloward and Lloyd Ohlin (1960). Their differential opportunity theory of delinquent subcultures was extremely important in the history of criminological and deviance theory, in that perhaps no other theory was responsible for generating so much government funding in the United States (DeKeseredy, Ellis, and Alvi, 2005). The logic was that if gang membership was a function of a lack of legitimate opportunity structures for youths, then the solution was to increase these opportunities. Under President Kennedy, and especially under President Johnson with his "War on Poverty" in the 1960s, a wide variety of programs were instituted to deal with educational deficiencies and job training. Unfortunately, under what Curran and Renzetti (2001) call the late President Reagan's "War on the Poor" in the 1980s, those programs not earlier eliminated by President Nixon were killed off, and today, there is still considerable resistance in the United States to implementing policies guided by Cloward and Ohlin, and others with similar perspectives on social problems.

Most sociologists who study crime, though, are what some criminologists would refer to as "liberal progressives." In other words, they: accept official definitions of crime (e.g., legal definitions); ignore concepts and theories offered by Marxist, feminist, critical race, and other "radical" scholars; call for fine-tuning state institutions' responses to social problems (e.g., expand the role of the welfare state); pay little – if any – attention to the role of broader social forces, and primarily use quantitative methods to collect and analyze crime and criminal justice data (Ratner, 1985).

Metaphorically speaking, critical criminologists, on the other hand, throw bricks through establishment or mainstream criminology's windows (Young, 1998). "[R]esolutely sociological in orientation" (Carrington and Hogg, 2008, p. 5), critical criminologists oppose official definitions of crime, official statistics (e.g., police arrest data), and positivism, but are for social justice, human rights, and the like (Stubbs, 2008). Positivism assumes that human behavior is determined and can be measured (Curran and Renzetti, 2001). Moreover, within the discipline of criminology, there is "an enduring commitment to measurement" (Hagan, 1985, p. 78).

The primary objective of this book is to provide readers with a brief scholarly overview of critical criminology, which has undergone many changes since its birth roughly 40 years ago. It is defining critical criminology that I turn to next.

DEFINITION OF CRITICAL CRIMINOLOGY

Although the term has been around since the early 1970s, many criminologists are still not exactly sure what the words *critical criminology* mean (DeKeseredy and Perry, 2006a). This applies not only to people who do not consider themselves critical criminologists, but also to people who actually feel that they are part of the tradition. Although various definitions have been proposed, there is no widely accepted precise formulation (Stubbs, 2008). However, for the purpose of this book, I offer a modified version of Jock Young's (1988) definition of radical criminology. Here, critical criminology is defined as a perspective that views the major sources of crime as the unequal class, race/ethnic, and gender relations that control our society. Certainly, as Schwartz and Hatty (2003) observe, "there are many types of critical criminology as there are writers and teachers in the area" (p. ix), and this book is specifically crafted to reflect this diversity.

Stubbs (2008), Carrington and Hogg (2008), Michalowski (1996), and others (e.g., DeKeseredy and Perry, 2006a) repeatedly note, there is no single critical criminology. Rather, there are critical criminologies that have different origins, use different methods, and that have diverse political beliefs. Nevertheless, as Friedrichs (2009) observes, "The unequal distribution of power or of material resources within contemporary societies provides a unifying point of departure for all strains of critical criminology" (p. 210). Another common feature all critical criminologists share is the rejection of solutions to crime measures such as "zero-tolerance" policing (e.g., criminalizing incivilities like panhandling), three-strikes sentencing, private prisons, coercive counseling therapy, and so on. Instead, critical criminologists regard major structural and cultural changes within society as essential steps to reduce crime and promote social justice.

Still, just because critical criminologists call for major economic, political, and cultural transformations does not mean that they totally disregard criminal justice reform, an issue of paramount concern to conservative scholars, politicians, journalists, and members of the general public. After all, every society requires a mixture of formal and informal means of social control (Michalowski, 1985). Still, the types of criminal justice reform called for do not include more punitive initiatives or hurtful forms of psychological treatment, such as the cruel electroshock "treatment" carried out in the 1950s in Montreal by Dr. Ewen Cameron at McGill University's Allan Memorial Institute. Funded by the Central Intelligence Agency (CIA), Cameron's unethical medical experiments also involved isolating people for weeks, keeping them asleep for lengthy periods of time, and the administration of "drug cocktails," including LSD and PCP. At least nine people who went to Cameron seeking relief from minor psychiatric problems (e.g., depression) ended up being used "without their knowledge and permission, as human guinea pigs to satisfy the CIA's thirst for information about how to control the human mind" (N. Klein, 2007, p. 31).

Some things don't change. As Naomi Klein (2007) vividly describes in her riveting book, *The Shock Doctrine: The Rise of Disaster Capitalism*, Cameron played a major role in creating recent US government torture techniques, such as those recently applied to inmates at Guantanamo. She notes:

> Indeed, in the testimonies, reports and photographs that have come out of Guantanamo, it is as if the Allan Memorial Institute of the 1950s had been transported to Cuba. When first detained, prisoners are put into intense sensory deprivation, with hoods, blackout goggles and heavy headphones to block out all sound. They are left in isolation cells for months, taken out only to have their senses bombarded with barking dogs, strobe light and endless tape loops of babies crying, music blaring and cats meowing.
>
> (p. 51)

Critical criminologists define the actions of Cameron and those who tortured inmates at Guantanamo as crimes. In addition, they call for progressive short-term policies that target the major social, political, cultural, and economic forces that propel people into crime, such as poverty, sexism, and deindustrialization. Of course, critical criminologists are not the only ones who call for such strategies. Recall that some initiatives informed by Cloward and Ohlin (1960), as well as other strain theorists (e.g., Merton, 1938), are also designed to maximize people's educational and employment opportunities. Consider that one new direction in critical criminology – left realism – is well known in the field for advancing strategies such as a higher minimum wage and state-sponsored, affordable, and quality health care (DeKeseredy, Alvi, and Schwartz, 2006).

Critical criminology has gone through many significant changes since its inception and it will continue to evolve because its proponents advance progress (DeKeseredy and Perry, 2006b). Still, just because something is "old" does not mean that it is no longer valuable. For example, nearly 15 years ago, in the introduction to their anthology, *Thinking Critically about Crime*, Brian MacLean and Dragan Milovanovic (1997a, p. 15) observed that, "far from being 'hegemonic,' and far from being monolithic in its thinking, critical criminology is a discipline characterized by a rich theoretical diversity." Trees with many branches have one trunk. Similarly, while there are different ways of thinking critically about crime, critical criminology has some important common characteristics, such as those described previously. In addition, critical criminologists disavow all criminologists as "neutral scientific experts" (Stubbs, 2008, p. 7). They also have no problem being labeled *political*. After all, as the famous French philosopher Jean Paul Sartre (1964) put it, "all writing is political" (p. 29), and critical criminologists want their work to help reduce much pain and suffering. Moreover, like many other contemporary social scientists, critical criminologists contend that no scientific method, theory, or policy is value free (DeKeseredy and Dragiewicz, 2007).

In one of the most widely read and cited social scientific articles in the world, Howard Becker (1967) asks sociologists, "Whose side are we on?" By now, most, if not all, readers have figured out that critical criminologists are on the side of the socially and economically excluded. Included in this group of "outsiders" (Becker, 1973) are victims of human-rights violations, those who lost jobs because corporations like General Motors moved operations to developing nations, people lacking adequate social services (e.g., health care and child care), and the targets of state terrorism, such as those imprisoned at Guantanamo (Schwendinger and Schwendinger, 1975; Tepperman, 2010). Critical criminologists want to broaden the definition of crime to include the harms listed above, as well as racism, sexism, imperialism, and corporate wrongdoings (Elias, 1986; Reiman and Leighton, 2010).

Kubrin, Stucky, and Krohn (2009) claim that the critical criminological "literature is characterized by too many ideas and not enough systematic research and that most empirical studies are illustrative of, but do not actually *test* the theory" (p. 239; emphasis in original). Nothing could be further from the truth. Another thing that brings critical criminologists together is years of in-depth research using a variety of methods, including ethnography, biography, narrative, deconstruction, and other qualitative methods (Lynch, Michalowski, and Groves, 2000). Phillipe Bourgois' (1995) study is an excellent example of pathbreaking critical criminological research that involved the collection of in-depth ethnographic data derived from five years spent in East Harlem (also referred to as El Barrio) observing, tape recording, and photographing various components of the lives of roughly 24 Puerto Rican crack dealers.

In some ways, Bourgois' work resembles that of Oscar Lewis' mid-1960s research (see his 1966 bestselling book, *La Vida*). For example, both scholars are anthropologists and both have done ethnographic research in El Barrio. However, they offer fundamentally different interpretations of the sources of poverty there and the myriad of social problems related to this highly injurious symptom of structured social inequality. Based on life-history data provided by one extended Puerto Rican family, Lewis' offering is the culture-of-poverty theory, which contends that middle-class and lower-class values are distinct. Instead of addressing how broader political, economic, and cultural forces are related to social and economic exclusion, he and more contemporary culture-of-poverty theorists argue that the poor are poor because, unlike middle-class people, they lack the moral fiber and discipline to get an education, to get jobs, defer gratification, and so on.

On the other hand, Bourgois' account asserts that macro-level factors such as the following have fueled the emergence of

Puerto Rican drug-dealing gangs in El Barrio: the rapid expansion of the finance, insurance, and real estate (FIRE) sector in New York City; the North American Free Trade Agreement (NAFTA); transnational corporations moving operations to make use of cheap labor; the implementation of high technology in the workplace; and the shift from a manufacturing to a service-based economy. Bourgois also contends that these ghetto-based criminal subcultures are not distinct from the wider or mainstream US culture. On the contrary, they are a core element of US culture and are actively involved in the pursuit of the "American Dream" and the respect garnered from it.

Bourgois argues:

> Like most other people in the United States, drug dealers and street criminals are scrambling to obtain their piece of the pie as fast as possible. In fact, in their pursuit of success they are even following the minute details of the classical Yankee model for upward mobility. They are aggressively pursuing careers as private entrepreneurs; they take risks, work hard, and pray for good luck. They are the ultimate rugged individualists braving an unpredictable frontier where fortune, fame, and destruction are all around the corner, where the enemy is ruthlessly hunted down and shot.
>
> (Bourgois, 1995, p. 326)

Although he does not specifically identify himself as an anomie, a subcultural, or as a left realist theorist, Bourgois' perspective is obviously heavily informed by the work of Albert Cohen (1955), Robert K. Merton (1938), Steven Messner and Richard Rosenfeld (2006), and Jock Young (1999). Note that left realists assert that inner-city people who lack legitimate means of solving the problem of relative deprivation come into contact with other frustrated disenfranchised people and form subcultures, which in turn encourage and legitimate criminal behaviors (Lea and Young, 1984). As Bourgois discovered, receiving respect from peers is highly valued among El Barrio males who are denied status in mainstream, middle-class society. Moreover, his work helps sensitize readers to how critical criminologists borrow some concepts and methods from mainstream scholars to help demonstrate how various types of inequality influence people to commit crime and to the ways in which these social forces affect societal reactions to crime and incivilities (DeKeseredy, in press b).

There is another problem with Kubrin *et al.*'s (2009) characterization of critical criminology. Critical criminology is not devoid of theory testing, and contrary to what many mainstream criminologists assert, there are groups of critical criminologists who use quantitative methods. For example, using nationwide representative sample survey data on woman abuse in university/college dating gathered in Canada, Martin D. Schwartz and I tested hypotheses derived from feminist theories, male-peer-support theory, and routine-activities theory (DeKeseredy and Schwartz, 1998; Schwartz and DeKeseredy, 1997). Moreover, as a "card carrying" critical criminologist, it was not until the early part of this decade that I conducted a purely qualitative study (see DeKeseredy and Schwartz, 2009).

DeKeseredy *et al.* (2003) provide another reason why people unfamiliar with critical criminological research should not assume that all critical scholars only use qualitative methods. Heavily informed by Jock Young's (1999) theoretical work on social and economic exclusion, feminist perspectives on woman abuse, and other progressive schools of thought, their project involved administering a victimization survey, in-depth interviews with public housing residents, and the analyses of available Canadian census tract and enumeration data.

There is much empirical diversity found in critical criminological literature, which reflects the view that research methods are tools that can be used in a variety of ways to achieve a variety of goals. Consider something as simple as a shovel. It can be used to build a shelter for the homeless and a private prison that houses and punishes poor victims of the US government's "war on drugs." Obviously, critical criminologists prefer using a shovel to build a shelter and use research methods to reveal how broader social forces contribute to crime and draconian means of social control (DeKeseredy and Perry, 2006a).

Prior to the mid-1980s, the objects of study for critical criminologists were mainly the ruling elite, corporate and white-collar criminals, law-breaking government officials, and the people who make the decisions on what is to be criminalized and what is not (DeKeseredy and Schwartz, 1996). Today, as described in more detail in Chapter 3, critical criminology involves the study of crime from all directions, including in the "suites," on the streets, and in domestic/household settings.

Since critical criminologists use a variety of empirical techniques and study a wide range of topics, it could easily be argued that many of these progressive scholars are interested in the same questions as other criminologists, such as: Why do people deal drugs or commit predatory street crimes? The most important difference is that they are not likely to look at flaws in the makeup of individuals, or study the "inherent" pathologies of particular groups, but rather they focus on the flaws in the makeup of a society that breeds, creates, and sustains such people (DeKeseredy and Perry, 2006a).

Theoretical and empirical work done by critical criminologists often involves "mixing and matching" (Schwartz and Hatty, 2003). In addition to borrowing concepts from mainstream theories, critical criminologists "create for themselves identities that cross over several subfields" of progressive thought and research (p. x), and these identities change according to the topics studied. For example, Martin Schwartz and I draw from left realism to explain inner-city predatory street crime and are guided by feminist and male-peer-support theories in our work on woman abuse. Rather than strictly adhere to one position, contemporary critical criminologists "are able to balance more than one belief at the same time" and often find that "an amalgam of two or more theories satisfies them intellectually" (Schwartz and Hatty, 2003, p. x).

In sum, then, the answer to the question "What do critical criminologists do?" is that they do many different empirical, theoretical, and political things. Still, as Elliott Currie (2008b) states in his brief commentary on the chapters included in Carrington and Hogg's (2008, p. vii) *Critical Criminology: Issues, Debates, Challenges*:

> There is no party line here; the contributors don't all speak with the same voice, but what links their diverse perspectives is a willingness to apply a critical lens not only to the work of their more conventional counterparts in the discipline but their own as well.

This can be said of all critical criminologists.

Critical criminology is definitely an intellectual movement (Michalowski, 1996), but it is much more than an academic enterprise. Included among critical criminology's diverse voices are people inside and outside the academy who devote the bulk or part of their energy and time to the progressive struggle for social change. For instance, in 2002, Lisa Simpson and two other plaintiffs filed a lawsuit against the University of Colorado. During a recruiting weekend, football players and recruits sexually assaulted them. In their lawsuit, the plaintiffs argued that there were previous assaults by players, the university was aware of these prior attacks, and that the university violated Title IX of the Education Amendments of 1972 by not acting to prevent further sexual assaults (Fleury-Steiner and Miller, 2008). This law states: "No person in the US shall, on the basis of sex, be excluded from participation in, be denied the benefits of, or be subjected to discrimination under any education program or activity receiving federal assistance" (US Department of Labor, 2009).

In 2005 a male judge dismissed the lawsuit. Needless to say, his decision was met with a giant outcry, especially among the feminist community, including members of the American Society of Criminology's Division on Women and Crime (DWC). Based at the University of Colorado at Boulder, feminist criminologist Joanne Belknap was among several people who helped the rape victims and she confronted and challenged the university's administration. Together with two colleagues, Belknap also created a consensual-sex training program for the University of Colorado's football team. Similar to many other women who challenge the patriarchal status quo, she experienced some of the vicious tactics of the anti-feminist backlash, such as threatening phone calls (Belknap, 2005; Fleury-Steiner and Miller, 2008).[3]

In honor of her activism, Belknap received the DWC's CoraMae Richey Mann "Inconvenient Woman of the Year" award, which "recognizes the scholar/activist who has participated in publicly promoting the ideals of gender equality and women's rights throughout society, particularly as it related to gender and crime issues." Like Belknap, Brian MacLean is another award-winning critical criminologist who helped stimulate social change. With two colleagues (Basran, Gill, and MacLean, 1995), he conducted a local Canadian survey of corporate violence against Punjabi farm-workers and their children. This study influenced Kwantlen University College and the British Columbia government to provide suitable and affordable child care for Punjabi farm-workers, and it is one of several empirically informed realistic solutions to unequal social conditions (Devine and Wright, 1993).

Over the past 30 years, critical criminology, as a discipline, has influenced many international organizations that struggle for social justice, including the Sentencing Project in the United States and Penal Reform International in England (Currie, 2008b). Critical criminologists are also members of such progressive organizations. For example, I serve on the Ohio Domestic Violence Network's advisory board and the California Coalition Against Sexual Assault's campus advisory board.

Nearly 30 years ago, critical criminology became institutionalized and established (Cohen, 1981). It is still this way today. As will be described in the next section of this chapter, we are witnessing what Jock Young (2008) observes as "the flourishing of critical criminology" (p. 259). However, even though critical criminologists have conducted pathbreaking studies, developed major theories, and proposed innovative ways of curbing crimes from all directions, many US criminologists, universities, politicians, criminal justice officials, members of the US general population, and even some textbook publishers are not receptive to their intellectual and political contributions. This is, of course, because they challenge the political, economic, and cultural status quo. To this day, many American critical criminologists experience hostility, academic isolation, and marginalization.

CRITICAL CRIMINOLOGY: A BRIEF HISTORY[4]

Critical criminology has its roots in what was once called *radical* criminology or *Marxist* criminology. Karl Marx himself said very little about crime (Schwartz and Hatty, 2003), but many critical criminologists, especially those who produced theories of crime and its control in the 1970s and early 1980s (e.g., Chambliss, 1975; Smandych, 1985; Spitzer, 1975), relied on Marxist analyses of capitalist society, and Taylor, Walton and Young's (1973) book, *The New Criminology: For a Social Theory of Deviance*, was especially important in the development of Marxist criminology (Matthews, 2003). Today, only a few critical criminologists identify themselves as Marxists, but the majority of them are concerned with class and how capitalism shapes crime, law, and social control (Schwartz and Hatty, 2003). Given the economic data presented at the start of this chapter and other symptoms of a global economic crisis, some critical criminologists correctly point out that "Marxism remains as relevant as ever for analyzing crime, criminal justice and the role of the state" (Russell, 2002, p. 113). For example, in the United States, Canada, and other capitalist countries, it is still primarily the socially and economically excluded who are incarcerated (De Giorgi, 2008; Wacquant, 2009). And, during this current period of staggering unemployment, like the "U.S. carceral archipelago," prisons around the world "swallow the growing number of people who do not compete on the regular labor market" (Hornqvist, 2008, p. 19). Of course, not everyone is equally likely to be a victim of violent crime, with those at the bottom of the socioeconomic ladder being at the highest risk (Currie, 2008a). For these and other reasons, then, critical criminologists are, to various extents, compelled to turn to Marx, "not because he is infallible, but because he is inescapable" (Heilbroner, 1980, p. 15).

Today, you will find critical criminologists around the world. However, the United States and the United Kingdom are the birthplaces of contemporary critical criminological thought (Sparks, 1980). Nevertheless, they have dissimilar academic histories. Although in the late 1960s and early 1970s academic sociologists were radicalized into the New Left in both the United Kingdom and the United States, the next steps were very different. In the United States, radicals rarely gained control over an entire department, and where they did – such as at the University of California (UC) at Berkeley – the result was more likely the disbanding of the department than the establishment of a beachhead of progressive theory, research, and praxis

(DeKeseredy and Schwartz, 1991a; Schwendinger, Schwendinger, and Lynch, 2008). Although isolated radicals have often been tolerated if they did not cause much trouble, radical criminologists and critical legal studies scholars have been heavily victimized by "academic McCarthyism" (Friedrichs, 1989). For example, the author of the widely read and cited 1969 book, *The Child Savers*, progressive criminologist Anthony Platt, was denied tenure at the UC at Berkeley in 1974 despite meeting the criteria of good teaching and excellent scholarship. At that time, the regents of the UC were conservative elites with major connections to the military–industrial complex, and they had the power to veto tenure recommendations (Schwendinger *et al.*, 2008). The UC at Berkeley chancellor was quoted as saying Platt was an "orthodox Marxist" and "biased in his teaching" (cited in Leonard, 1974, p. 1).

Fueled by extraordinary funding from the Law Enforcement Assistance Administration of the US Department of Justice for tuition scholarships for law-enforcement personnel, the main drive in US academic life was to found departments of criminal justice. With the majority of the students in these programs often either in-service or pre-service law enforcement, the major subject matter taught was commonly administrative criminology[5] and technical law enforcement. To staff hundreds of departments starting almost simultaneously, many schools hired line personnel from police and corrections agencies with limited training in academic criminology. In later years, these faculty duplicated themselves by requiring line experience in law enforcement for new faculty (DeKeseredy and Schwartz, 1991a).

As an obvious result, the curriculum focused on conservative "law and order" criminology and technical law enforcement. Students were primarily taught that crime is a property of the individual (the biological/psychological orientation), and that the most effective ways of dealing with criminals were to "police 'em, jail 'em [and maybe even] kill 'em" (Barak, 1986, p. 201). Although, to be sure, many radicals still taught courses in criminology or the sociology of deviant behavior, these courses were often marginalized to the edges of the discipline or only taught in sociology departments as electives for sociology majors. At the same time, enormous sums of money were available to criminologists doing research in administrative criminology, particularly studies designed to improve efficiency in criminal justice system operations (DeKeseredy and Schwartz, 1996).

Today, many US textbooks also marginalize critical criminologists. For example, most of the major criminology texts published each year in the United States purport to present a balanced view of the many conflicting theories within criminology. In fact, virtually none do, and perhaps this is an impossible goal to achieve. However, one area that is consistently given poor treatment is critical criminology. Some texts simply ignore this side of the field. Others give extensive coverage, perhaps an entire chapter, but limit themselves to ancient intellectual battles and detailed coverage of long-discredited leftist theories.

Even the prestigious American Society of Criminology (ASC) has a history of being unkind to critical criminologists. For instance, in 1979, some mainstream criminologists attacked radical criminologists in a special issue of *Criminology* (volume 16, Number 4, February 1979),[6] which is one of two official journals of the ASC. According to Schwendinger *et al.* (2008, p. 55): "This edition, devoted to radical criminology, was unprecedented. It was the first time any professional society had published a separate edition of its official journal aimed at discrediting an up-and-coming theoretical and policy perspective in the field." Nevertheless, events such as this have not stopped US critical criminologists in their tracks. Critical criminology is very much alive and well in the United States, as it is in the United Kingdom, Canada, and other countries.

The situation was quite different in the United Kingdom, where deviance courses were taught by sociology departments, and often by instructors affiliated with the National Deviance Conference. Radicals established "power bases" in various polytechnics (e.g., Middlesex, which was the "home" of left realists), universities, and colleges of education (Young, 1988). Since scholars such as those belonging to the left realist cohort were able to work in close proximity to each other, it is not surprising that united schools of thought were able to develop in the United Kingdom. One of the more recent of these is cultural criminology (Ferrell, Hayward, and Young, 2008), which is a major intellectual movement at the University of Kent in the United Kingdom – the home of the "cultural criminology team."

Another major difference is the effect that scholars have had outside the ivory towers of the academy. As with socialists and feminists generally, American radical criminologists have been marginalized on every level. Not only was there no national radical conference founded, but it was not until 1988 that radical criminologists felt strong enough to begin to work toward institutionalizing themselves as a division within the ASC (DeKeseredy and Schwartz, 1991a; Michalowski, 1996).

In the United Kingdom, critical criminological discourse has influenced Labour Party politics, especially at the local level in the 1980s, when Young (1988, p. 170) wrote:

> [a] new wave of young Labour politicians, many of them schooled in the New Left Orthodoxy of the sixties, were brought into power in the inner-city Labour strongholds. They – and in particular the police committee support units which they brought into being – became important political focuses for the ideas and concerns of radical criminology.

At the time Young made this statement, the connection between politicians and academics provided opportunities that were rarely available in the United States. Although, just as in the United States, the Home Office provided research grants only to administrative criminologists, the opportunity existed for radical criminologists to work through Labour-controlled local government offices. Further, there was no political group in the United States similar to the British Labour Party or the Canadian New Democratic Party, where socialists and other progressives were drawn to participate in mainstream political activities. To a small extent, the US Democratic Party adheres to some socialist principles, but that remains a slight variation with a dominant order committed to perpetuating and legitimating capitalist, patriarchal social relations (DeKeseredy, 2007; Miliband, 1969). Unfortunately, despite the popularity of President Barak Obama, we are already witnessing many Democrats adopting an approach Elliott Currie (1992) defined nearly 20 years ago as "progressive retreatism." This involves embracing parts of conservative policies to win elections. Furthermore, many critics now claim that the British Labour Party has lost its bearings and now resembles the US Republican Party.

Democratic Party meetings do not bring US radicals together to formulate agendas such as left realism, because their voices are likely to be ignored. Historically, the Democratic Party has not provided research opportunities for radical criminologists, even at the most local levels. However, during Bill Clinton's term as President of the United States, and since the passing of the 1994 Violence Against Women Act, a sizeable portion of research grants were given to feminist scholars by the US Justice Department to study key issues related to violence against women. For example, while I was based at Ohio University from 2000 to 2004, I received such a grant to conduct a qualitative study of separation/divorce sexual assault in rural Ohio – a project that was heavily informed by feminist theory and involved the use of feminist research methods (DeKeseredy and Schwartz, 2009).

In sum, political and academic forces have indirectly contributed to the development of a more united group of critical criminologists in the United Kingdom. Operating within more repressive political and academic contexts, US critical criminologists, until relatively recently, were forced to "go it alone." Their individual contributions, however, are important and warrant attention.

As stated previously, US criminology textbooks commonly devote little attention to critical scholarship beyond, say, a few brief statements on Taylor, Walton, and Young's (1973) *The New Criminology*. Further, most of these texts pay little, if any, attention to the critical work done in other countries such as Canada, Australia, Italy, Norway, Venezuela, and France, despite the fact that critical criminologists based there are engaged in pathbreaking scholarship, activism, and policy development. This cross-cultural or international approach is missing even in widely cited US critical texts, such as Lynch *et al.*'s (2000) *The New Primer in Radical Criminology*.

In Canada, where I live, while critical criminology may not be a core component of the broader Canadian criminology curriculum, critical criminologists are much more likely to hold tenured positions at prominent universities. This is due, in part, to the fact that progressive ways of studying and thinking about a host of social problems are highly respected in sociology departments. Further, Canada is witnessing a growth in new criminology programs, some of which include a large number of critical criminologists. For example, in the winter of 2010, approximately 11 critical criminologists were affiliated with the University of Ontario Institute of Technology's (UOIT) Faculty of Criminology, Justice, and Policy Studies. Moreover, *Critical Criminology*, the official journal of the ASC's Division on Critical Criminology (DCC) was also based at UOIT.

Critical criminology is an international enterprise and new information technologies make it easier for critical criminologists to exchange ideas with their peers based outside their respective countries and to develop collaborative projects. Nevertheless, much more needs to be done to develop a more inclusive critical criminology, one that routinely involves including scholarly work produced outside primarily English-speaking countries in books such as this one (DeKeseredy and Perry, 2006a). This will eventually happen because critical criminology is a never-ending and constantly evolving way of "doing criminology" (Lynch *et al.*, 2000).

Rural crime has ranked among the least studied social problems in criminology (DeKeseredy, Donnermeyer, Schwartz, Tunnell, and Hall, 2007). As Donnermeyer, Jobes, and Barclay (2006, p. 199) put it in their comprehensive review of rural crime research:

> If rural crime was considered at all, it was a convenient "ideal type" contrasted with the criminogenic conditions assumed to exist exclusively in urban locations. Rural crime was rarely examined, either comparatively with urban crime or a subject of investigation in its own right.

Critical criminology, too, is guilty of devoting selective inattention to rural issues (Donnermeyer and DeKeseredy, 2008). However, today there is a growth in critical criminological analyses of rural crime and societal reactions to it, such as the work of Hogg and Carrington (2006) in Australia, DeKeseredy and Schwartz's (2009) feminist research on separation/divorce sexual assault in rural Ohio, and UK scholars Chakraborti and Garland's (2004) contribution to a critical understanding of rural racism. Judith Grant's (2008) feminist analysis of Appalachian Ohio women's pathways from addiction to recovery is another important contribution to the field. Moreover, heavily influenced by Taylor *et al.*'s (1973) *New Criminology* and by research on "gendered violence and the architecture of rural life" (Hogg and Carrington, 2006, p. 171), Donnermeyer and DeKeseredy (2008) outline some key elements of a new or critical rural criminology that does not privilege class over gender.

Of course, the critical criminological project will always be incomplete, which is a blessing rather than a curse. Critical criminologists fully recognize that resisting change, or advancing standardization of theory, method, and policy "is the parent of stagnation" (Jacobs, 2004, p. 119; see also DeKeseredy and Perry, 2006a).

THE CURRENT STATE OF CRITICAL CRIMINOLOGY[7]

Twenty-five years after the publication of *The New Criminology*, two of its co-authors, Paul Walton and Jock Young (1988, p. vii) stated that:

> Radical criminology ... has since proliferated, developed and flourished. The various currents that form its past, whether Marxist, radical feminist or anarchist, continue in fierce dispute but have in common the notion that crime and the present day processes of criminalization are rooted in the core structures of society, whether its class nature, its patriarchal form or its inherent authoritarianism.

What they said then is true today. As is frequently pointed out, critical criminology is even stronger than when Walton and Young published their seminal anthology, *The New Criminology Revisited* (DeKeseredy and Perry, 2006a). For example, the ASC's DCC now has nearly 400 members, many of whom are based outside the United States and the United Kingdom. Again, with the help of 30 editorial board members from around the world, the DCC publishes *Critical Criminology: An International Journal*, and this progressive collective also produces a quarterly newsletter, *The Critical Criminologist*. A website (www.critcrim.org) is also a valuable source of information for DCC members and others interested in the topics covered in this book and elsewhere.

The DCC is one of only five divisions of the ASC and overlaps with three of the ASC's strongest divisions: the Division on Women and Crime; the Division of International Criminology; and the Division on People of Color and Crime. Also consider that one of the pioneers of critical criminology, William Chambliss, was the president of the ASC and the Society for the Study of Social Problems (SSSP), arguably the second most important organization in sociology. Stephen Pfohl, a postmodern criminologist and deviance theorist, succeeded him as president of the SSSP in the early 1990s. Moreover, Robert Bohm, another widely cited critical criminologist, served as president of the Academy of Criminal Justice Sciences (the national US association for criminal justice scholars and practitioners), and Jeffery Walker held this position in 2006.

There are dozens of other examples of critical criminologists who have held key positions, such as annual meeting or major committee chairs. Critical criminologists also routinely serve on the editorial boards of "mainstream" journals, such as *Criminology, Justice Quarterly*, and *Crime and Delinquency*. The key point is this: critical criminologists are a major part of the broader academic criminological community and, as you will discover from reading subsequent chapters of this book, they have made many important theoretical, empirical, and political contributions to the field.

Returning to where this chapter started, many would agree with Jock Young's (1988, p. 293) statement that "If there ever was a need for a new criminology, it is now...." The world is facing a terrifyingly long list of problems, including the proliferation of violent, racist pornography (DeKeseredy and Olsson, in press; Jensen, 2007), new forms of global violence (Currie, 2008b), human-rights violations and genocide (Tepperman, 2010), and the "rise of disaster capitalism" (N. Klein, 2007).

To make matters worse, more US citizens die of homicide every three months than the number of people killed by the September 11 terrorist attacks on the World Trade Center in New York and in the Iraq War as of 2008 (Currie, 2008a). Staying the course has done little, if anything, to make the world safer from violence and related harms. Isn't it time to think critically about crime?[8]

2

CONTEMPORARY CRITICAL CRIMINOLOGICAL SCHOOLS OF THOUGHT

It is important that we recognize that each of the many critical criminologies existing today address some portion of the "intersecting social relations that are fundamental to the study of crime and justice" (Barak, 1995, p. 6). If we keep this in mind, we will all move closer to fulfilling the liberative potential of critical criminology.

(Michalowski, 1996, p. 15)

Often referred to incorrectly by mainstream scholars as "conflict theories" (e.g., Kubrin, Stucky, and Krohn, 2009), critical criminological perspectives on crime, law, and social control are repeatedly accused of focusing "more on a critique of the shortcomings of other criminologists than on offering an alternative explanation of crime" (Akers and Sellers, 2004, p. 237). In addition, as stated in Chapter 1, critical criminologists are frequently criticized for not actually testing theories. There are some major problems with these assertions and since the second claim was responded to earlier (see Chapter 1), the first one will be briefly addressed here. Critical criminologists have devoted (and continue to devote) much time and energy to exposing the weaknesses of mainstream scholars' work (Schwartz, 1991), but so do all criminological theorists. In fact, almost every theory text includes critiques of every theory reviewed by the authors. Criminology, in general, is characterized by much debate, and mainstream criminologists are among the first to point out flaws in their colleagues' writings and research.

Contrary to what many conservative scholars state, critical criminologists are actively involved in developing alternative theories. True, there was a time when most progressives directed much, if not all, of their attention to Marxist analyses of the class-based nature of the origins and functions of law and, for the most part, ignored addressing the causes of interpersonal crimes, such as those committed by poor people in urban ghettos. Martin Schwartz (1991, p. 119) recalls:

> Many of us were sort of idealists 20 years ago. We were outraged that the state only saw crime in the actions of African-American and poor youth. In Albert K. Cohen's terms, some of us were "negativistic" – if James Q. Wilson[1] says yes, then I say no. There was some rooting for the underdog and great concern that any actions against the underdog were giving succor to the "Great Enemy."

There are still critical criminologists who theorize the role of the state and law and how they are biased against those at the bottom of the socioeconomic ladder (e.g., Reiman and Leighton, 2010). Such work is much needed because corporate crime is endemic to capitalist societies, and good theories on this problem help us find effective solutions. As Kurt Lewin (1951), the founder of modern social psychology, correctly pointed out, "There is nothing so practical as a good theory" (p. 169). The same can be said of good theories of street crime, violence against women behind closed doors, hate crime, and a myriad of other harms. Critical criminologists recognize this, and since the late 1980s, a growing mass of them have crafted and tested theories of interpersonal victimization.

One of the main objectives of this chapter, then, is to challenge the myth that contemporary critical criminological perspectives are simply "rhetorical" (Wheeler, 1976), "ideologically charged ideas" (Liska, 1987), and are "untestable" (Akers and

Sellers, 2004). At first glance, some readers might perceive two of the above citations as old and consider that the claims associated with them are no longer in vogue. They are still widely cited in popular textbooks (see, for example, Kubrin *et al.*, 2009) because criminology is still dominated by mainstream thinking and a reluctance to seriously engage with the left.

The second, and equally important, objective of this chapter is to briefly review some major contemporary critical schools of thought. I hasten to mention that this overview is by no means not exhaustive and that the order in which each perspective appears does not reflect a hierarchy of importance. Even more offerings will be created by the time you finish reading this book because critical criminologists have a deep-rooted and ongoing commitment to doing theoretical work that meets the highest contemporary disciplinary standards.

FEMINISM[2]

As noted before, many critical criminologists, especially those who produced theories of crime and its control in the 1970s and early 1980s (e.g., Chambliss and Seidman, 1982; Pearce, 1976; Quinney, 1974), relied on Marxist analyses of capitalist society. Although important and pathbreaking, these perspectives were "gender-blind" (Gelsthorpe and Morris, 1988). Even Taylor, Walton, and Young's (1973) *The New Criminology*, perhaps the most important work of its generation, ignores women and gender. Of course, this criticism can just as easily be leveled against the overwhelming majority of mainstream criminologists, including those considered pioneers in the field. For example, in his book *Causes of Delinquency*, eminent social control theorist Travis Hirschi (1969) states in a footnote that "in the analysis that follows the 'non-negro' becomes 'white' and the girls disappear" (pp. 35–36). Many who followed in Hirschi's footsteps also used all-male samples (Curran and Renzetti, 1994).

It should be noted in passing that over 30 years later, a re-analysis of the Richmond Youth Project data used in his study reveals that perceived racial discrimination is a powerful predictor of delinquency.[3] According to the scholars who revisited this data set, "Hirschi missed a historic opportunity to focus the attention of a generation of criminologists on how the unique experiences of African Americans may shape their criminality" (Unnever, Cullen, Mathers, McClure, and Allison, 2009, p. 378).

It is often said: "That was then and this is now." As Chesney-Lind and Pasko (2004, p. 15) put it, "One might want to believe that such cavalier androcentrism is no longer found in academic approaches to delinquency." Alas, it still exists, even among some relatively new directions in critical criminology. Consider Roger Matthews' (2009) "re-fashioned" left realism that "prioritizes the role of theory" (p. 344). The word "gender" appears only once in the main text of his article and the words "feminism" and "patriarchy" are nowhere to be found (DeKeseredy and Schwartz, in press). From a feminist standpoint, then, contrary to what Matthews claims, his re-fashioned realist criminology is "more of the same" and does not move beyond what US left realist Elliott Currie (2007) refers to as "so what? criminology." Such criminology involves doing a-theoretical, quantitative research on relatively minor issues and presenting the findings in an unintelligible fashion. Jock Young (2004) labels this approach "voodoo criminology."

Much of criminology ignores women and girls in conflict with the law or simply treats sex as a variable to be included in complex statistical analyses, but the last two decades have witnessed an "outpouring of feminist scholarship" (Daly and Chesney-Lind, 1988). Moreover, the American Society of Criminology's (ASC) Division on Women and Crime (DWC), like the ASC's Division on Critical Criminology (DCC), is one of the ASC's strongest divisions and the vast majority of its members publicly identify themselves as feminist scholars. Furthermore, the DWC is now close to 30 years old and its members have made many outstanding empirical, theoretical, and political contributions to the field.

Defining feminism is not an easy task. Still, one thing leading experts in the field all agree with is that "feminism is not merely about adding women onto the agenda" (Currie and MacLean, 1993, p. 6). For the purpose of this book, I offer Kathleen Daly and Meda Chesney-Lind's (1988) definition, which is still one of the most widely used and cited offerings. Throughout this book, "feminism" refers to "a set of theories about women's oppression and a set of strategies for change" (Daly and Chesney-Lind, 1988, p. 502). Nevertheless, it is incorrect to paint all feminists with the same brush because there are at least 12 variants of feminist criminological theory (Maidment, 2006). However, all feminists prioritize gender, which should not be confused with sex even though both terms are often incorrectly used interchangeably. Gender is the "sociocultural and psychological shaping, patterning, and evaluating of female and male behavior" (Schur, 1984, p. 10). Sex, on the other hand, refers to the biologically based categories of "female" and "male," which are stable across history and cultures (Dragiewicz, 2009). For example, violent crimes are committed mainly by men, but many societies have much lower rates of violence than those of the United States, the Russian Federation, or Columbia (Currie, 2008a; Krug, Dahlberg, and Mercy, 2002). So, if "boys will be boys," they "will be so differently" (Kimmel, 2000), depending on where they live, their peer groups, social class position and race, and a host of other factors (DeKeseredy and Schwartz, in press; Messerschmidt, 1993).

Most feminists also agree that the United States, the United Kingdom, Canada, and many other countries are patriarchal societies (DeKeseredy and Schwartz, 1996; Ogle and Batton, 2009). There are conflicting definitions of patriarchy and it is a heavily contested concept (Hunnicutt, 2009), but it is not uncommon to follow scholars such as Dobash and Dobash (1979), who assert that patriarchy consists of two key elements: a structure and an ideology. Structurally, the patriarchy is a hierarchical organization in which males have more power and privilege than women. Certainly, North America is well known for being a continent characterized by gross gender inequity. For example, laws in 30 US states allow a man to receive conditional exemptions if he rapes his wife (Bergen, 2006).[4] Moreover, in Canada, on October 27, 2009, federal Liberal Member of Parliament Caroline Bennett, physician and former Public Health Minister, was heckled and shouted down by male members of the ruling Progressive Conservative Party when she tried to raise the issue of what kind of swine flu vaccination pregnant women should be taking (Delacourt, 2009). On

October 3, 2006, the same government announced that Status of Women Canada (SWC) is no longer eligible for funding for advocacy, government lobbying, or research projects. Further, SWC was required to delete the word "equality" from its list of goals (Carastathis, 2006).

Why do men maintain this power? Why don't most women rebel against their subordinate position? The answer is the other part of patriarchy: the ideology. The ideology of patriarchy provides a political and social rationale for itself. Both men and women come to believe that it is "natural" and "right" that women be in inferior positions. Men feel completely supported in excluding women, and up to a point, women feel their exclusion is correct (DeKeseredy and Schwartz, 1993). To someone (male or female) who believes completely in the ideology of patriarchy, the entire concept of equal rights or women's liberation is a pretty difficult topic, sounding not only wrong but unnatural – literally, it goes against nature (Schwartz and DeKeseredy, 1997).

This sounds fairly simple, and in fact most definitions of patriarchy are fairly simple. There are, though, varieties of patriarchy (Hunnicutt, 2009). For example, many feminist scholars focus on *social patriarchy*, which refers to the type of male domination at the societal level, as discussed above. A subsystem of social patriarchy, often called *familial patriarchy*, refers to male control in domestic or intimate settings (Barrett, 1985; Eisenstein, 1980; Ursel, 1986). These two components cannot be pulled too far apart and one variant cannot be fully understood without reference to the other (DeKeseredy and Schwartz, 2009; Smith, 1990).

It is beyond the scope of this book to examine all the different feminist perspectives on crime, law, and social control. In fact, there are many books on feminist approaches to understanding these issues. Nevertheless, it must be emphasized that feminist criminologists do extensive theoretical work on a myriad of important problems, including female gangs, violence against women, women and girls' pathways to crime, drugs, and moral panics about female youth violence. Further, feminist theorists and researchers alike have had a major impact on criminal justice policy (Lilly, Cullen, and Ball,

2007). For instance, due in large part to the efforts of feminist scholars, police departments and other criminal justice agencies no longer simply ignore women who are physically and sexually abused behind closed doors by their current or former male partners (DeKeseredy, Ellis, and Alvi, 2005).[5] Yet, since feminist theoretical work challenges "male-centered" ways of explaining deviance, crime, and social control, it is constantly challenged and often ridiculed by conservative students, practitioners, and academics.

For example, psychologist Donald Dutton (2006) accuses feminists of "dogma preservation" (p. ix), of "politically conceptualizing" domestic violence (p. xi), and of attempting to "spin" data to be consistent with their "paradigm" (p. 349). Dutton is also among a large group of conservative critics who claim that feminists only offer single-factor explanations of crime that focus exclusively on patriarchy. These are not legitimate criticisms. After all, no social scientific theory, method, or policy proposal is value-free (Harding, 1987). Moreover, as stated before, there is more than one feminist perspective on crime, law, and social control. Although *some* feminists claim that patriarchy is the direct cause of women's victimization, offending, or societal reactions to their behaviors, there is a large feminist literature combining both macro- and micro-level factors, such as unemployment, globalization, deindustrialization, life-events stress, intimate relationship status, familial and societal patriarchy, substance use, and other factors (DeKeseredy and Dragiewicz, 2007). In fact, feminists are among the most critical of single-factor explanations of female victimization or rule-breaking (DeKeseredy *et al.*, 2005).[6]

Feminist criminologists have also been accused of making "no attempt to operationalize patriarchy" (Ogle and Batton, 2009, p. 171), which is an erroneous claim. For instance, the late Michael D. Smith (1990) conducted a representative sample survey of woman abuse in Toronto and measured female respondents' perceptions of their intimate male partners' adherence to the ideology of familial patriarchy. For the purpose of his study, relevant themes of this ideology are an insistence on women's obedience, respect, loyalty, dependency, sexual access, and sexual fidelity (Barrett and McIntosh, 1982; Dobash and Dobash, 1979;

Pateman, 1988). Smith operationalized these themes with two indices. One index measured patriarchal beliefs, and the other measured patriarchal attitudes. DeKeseredy and Schwartz (1998) also administered these indices to men in the Canadian national survey of woman abuse in university/college dating. Cronbach's alpha coefficients (0.79 for beliefs and 0.76 for attitudes) show that these indicators are reliable and consistent with Smith's (1990) item factor analysis of female respondents (0.79 and 0.71, respectively).

Questions about patriarchal control are also used in qualitative studies of woman abuse. For example, DeKeseredy and Schwartz (2009) asked 43 rural Ohio women if their male ex-partners felt that men should be in charge at home. Of these women, 79 percent answered affirmatively. For example, one respondent said that her ex-husband, "wanted to be in control. He was in control for us, or you know I felt it." Similarly, another woman reported that her ex-partner "was the type of person where women were lower than men. And men were able, you know – women had to do what men told them. Which is pretty much my whole relationship with him" (p. 71). In sum, there is growing evidence refuting the claim that "patriarchy is difficult to measure as an independent variable" (Lilly *et al.*, 2007, p. 217).

Another criticism offered by some feminist criminologists is that much of feminist criminology "focuses narrowly" on women's victimization (Miller, 2003), which gives the "false impression that women have only been victims, they have never successfully fought back, and that women cannot be effective social agents on behalf of themselves or others" (Harding, 1987, p. 5). This is a rather dated criticism because we now see a major growth in feminist work on women's criminality and key factors associated with it, including neighborhood disadvantage (Caputo, 2008), the feminization of poverty (Morash, 2006; Steffensmeier and Streifel, 1992), and childhood abuse (Chesney-Lind, 2001). Moreover, heavily influenced by life-course theories, some feminist scholars examine female pathways in and out of criminal behavior (Morash, 2006). One recent example is Judith Grant's (2008) work on marginalized rural Ohio women's pathways to recovery from substance abuse.

In addition, feminist research shows that most women in abusive relationships or in nonviolent intimate unions characterized by other means of patriarchal dominance and control are not weak people unable to take steps on their own behalf and on that of their children (DeKeseredy and Schwartz, 2009). Moreover, most battered women eventually leave abusive men, but separation or divorce alone often does not make them safer (Schwartz, 1989; Sev'er, 2002).[7] Still, there is ample evidence of what Morash (2006, p. 145) refers to as "victims exercising agency."

Feminist theories offer an alternative gendered way of thinking about crime (Vold, Bernard, and Snipes, 2002). So, too, does another school of thought heavily influenced by feminism – masculinities (Gardiner, 2005; Messerschmidt, 2005). The study of masculinities is the gendered study of men (Morgan, 1992), and masculinities theories of crime are examined below.

MASCULINITIES THEORIES[8]

Men commit most crimes, especially violent offences, but this does not mean that all men are criminal and that male crime does not vary across countries, regions, socioeconomic groups, and so on. In fact, certain societies are much more likely than others to teach violence to men (Hottocks, 1994). For example, World Health Organization homicide data show that men's risk of committing murder in Colombia is much higher than it is in Japan or France, which have the lowest rate of homicide deaths in the world (Krug et al., 2002). Further, Oakland, California's population was 375,000 in 2006, but had many more homicides than Sweden, which had a population of nine million at that time (Currie, 2008a). Furthermore, homicide is a relatively infrequent crime and thus "we are not talking about a tendency that is either universal or inevitable" (Newburn and Stanko, 1994, p. 4).

A central argument of masculinities theorists is that there is no simple standard of being a man that guides all male behavior, including crime (Messerschmidt, 1993; Polk, 2003). Although society functions in many ways to promote male violence, there remains in any situation other means of expressing one's masculinity (Connell, 2000). For example, it is well known that professional hockey players can be exceptionally violent; yet, some hockey players will not fight an opponent because they can "do masculinity" in other ways. A prime example is Wayne Gretzky, who holds the record for the most goals scored in the National Hockey League. Gretzky rarely fought. His amazing ability to score goals and help his teams win games and championships were key resources at his disposal to demonstrate he was "manly" (DeKeseredy and Schwartz, 2005a). Those lacking his skills, but under intense pressure from employers, teammates, and spectators to fight opponents who challenge them, commonly feel that they would be derided as of "doubtful moral worth" and "relatively useless to the team" (Smith, 1983, p. 42) if they walked away from violent "honor contests" (Polk, 2003).

Connell (1995) developed the basic vocabulary that many masculinities theorists use. He contends that in most areas there is one *hegemonic* masculinity, which is the dominant form. In the United States, Hollywood movie actors such as Vin Diesel, Sylvester Stallone, or Arnold Schwarzenegger (who became the Governor of California) best exemplify such masculinity. The basic components of hegemonic masculinity are: (1) avoid all things feminine; (2) restrict emotions severely; (3) show toughness and aggression; (4) exhibit self-reliance; (5) strive for achievement and status; (6) exhibit no relational attitudes toward sexuality; and, (7) actively engage in homophobia (Connell and Messerschmidt, 2005; Schwartz and DeKeseredy, 1997; Weitzer and Kubrin, 2009). Masculinities studies show that men are encouraged to live up to these ideals and are sanctioned for not doing so, but that crime is just one of many ways of "doing gender" in a culturally specific way (Sinclair, 2002; West and Zimmerman, 1987). Moreover, masculinities theories remind us that the decision to commit certain crimes is affected by class and race relations that structure the resources available to accomplish what men feel provides their masculine identities (DeKeseredy and Schwartz, 2005a; Messerschmidt, 1997).

For example, many economically and socially marginalized young men, regardless of their ethnic/cultural background, are unable to accomplish masculinity at school through academic achievement, participation in sports, or involvement in extra-curricular activities (Messerschmidt, 1993). This problem results in some boys experiencing status frustration, dropping out of school, and creating a subculture with other boys who share their frustration (Cohen, 1955). This subculture grants members status based on accomplishing gender through violence and other illegitimate means (DeKeseredy and Schwartz, 2005a).

Many inner-city boys of color are not only denied masculine status through the inability to succeed in school, but also through unemployment due to deindustrialization and institutional racism (Hagedorn, 1998; Wilson and Taub, 2008). Numerous Hispanic and Asian young men experience similar problems. Thus, it is not surprising that members of these socially marginalized ethnic groups compose most of the street gangs in North America (M. Klein, 2007). It is not, of course, their skin color that contributes to a higher proportion of these social groups in gangs. Rather, it is what Currie (2008a) refers to as the "historical legacy of discrimination" that disproportionately subjects ethnic minority groups to the "social and economic disadvantages that tend to breed violence" (p. 69).

Corporate masculinity is distinct from masculinities found in schools, on the street, on assembly lines, in the family, and elsewhere. Instead of relying on violence, being a corporate "real man" entails "calculation and rationality as well as struggle for success, reward, and corporate recognition" (Messerschmidt, 1993, p. 136). Male executives compete with each other and measure masculinity according to their success in the business community. Corporate crime, then, is one technique of advancing this "gendered strategy of action."

Uncertain and competitive markets, fluctuating sales, government regulations, and relations with unions all obstruct corporate attempts to increase profits legitimately (Box, 1983; DeKeseredy et al., 2005). Masculinities theorist James Messerschmidt (1993) asserts that these obstacles also threaten white corporate executive masculinity. Thus, corporate crime is a solution to both of these problems. That is, illegal and unethical practices are techniques of re-establishing or maintaining a particular type of masculinity, as well as profit margins.

Masculinities play a role in facilitating men's crime in many more arenas. In fact, there are various forms of masculinities (Connell, 1995; Hatty, 2000), which helps to explain the wide range of responses to the contemporary crises facing men. Among these areas are racist violence and homophobic violence ("gay bashing"). Following Connell (1987), Perry (2003) argues that these harms are linked to white men's desire to assert their superiority and dominance, as well as to the desire to "prove the very essence of their masculinity: heterosexuality" (p. 158). She further asserts that many men do not view such violence as breaking a cultural norm (on violence) as much as affirming "a culturally approved hegemonic masculinity: aggression, domi- nation, and heterosexuality" (p. 158). Of course, men engage in masculinist discourse to justify and allow their own violence in many other areas (DeKeseseredy and Schwartz, 2005a).

Numerous theories attempt to lay out which offender charac- teristics best predict crime, but the most powerful determinant is whether the offender is male (Schwartz and Hatty, 2003). It is not because of biological composition or factors identified by evolutionary psychologists (e.g., Daly and Wilson, 1988).[9] Mas- culinities theories remind us that men are not naturally aggres- sive. As Katz and Chambliss (1991) discovered through an in-depth review of the research on the relationship between biology and crime:

> An individual learns to be aggressive in the same manner that he or she learns to inhibit aggression. One is not a natural state, and the other culturally imposed: both are within our biological potential. Violence, sexism and racism are biological only in the sense that they are within the range of possible human attitudes and behaviors. But nonviolence, equality and justice are also biologically possible.
>
> (p. 270)

On top of motivating criminologists to pay more careful attention to "maleness" and its relationship to crime, masculin- ities theorists such as Messerschmidt (1993) and Mullins (2006) draw attention to how the intersection of race/ethnicity, class, and gender shape men's involvement in crime (Lilly et al., 2007). Even so, as Connell (2000, p. 82) puts it, "masculinities are not the whole story" about crime. Obviously, there are many other sources of crime. Mullins (2006), among others (e.g., Miller, 2002), correctly point outs, to simply argue that crime "is a way for men to 'do gender' or construct a masculine identity is of no theoretical import for understanding the etiological connections between masculinity and crime, and often obscures more than it illuminates" (Mullins, 2006, p. 19). Still, crime and its reduction cannot be adequately understood without an in-depth understanding of masculinities (Messerschmidt, 2005).

LEFT REALISM[10]

Since its birth in the mid-1980s, left realism has been sharply attacked from the right and the left. For example, according to mainstream criminologist Don Gibbons (1994, p. 170), it "can be best described as a general perspective centred on injunctions to 'take crime seriously' rather than as a well-developed theoretical perspective." Similarly, critical criminologist Stuart Henry (1999) claims that left realists offer a "limited conception of criminal etiology" (p. 139). It is also often said that left realism has "nothing new to say" and that it is no longer a major subdiscipline of critical criminology (DeKeseredy and Schwartz, 2005b). Contrary to what some critics state, left realism is not dormant and has the potential to be just as vibrant now as it was during the Reagan and Thatcher years when it was born. In fact, left realism has been "rediscovered" by Roger Matthews (2009), one of its British founders. The concepts of class, the state, and structure are emphasized in his recent attempt to foster the creation of a "coherent critical realist approach" to explaining crime and punishment (p. 341). On the other side of the Atlantic Ocean, North American left realists Walter DeKeseredy and Martin Schwartz (in press), as well as Elliott Currie (2004), also offer new left realist theories to be briefly summarized later in this section.

Left realists are concerned about the damage done by the crimes of the powerful (e.g., corporate and state crime), but the bulk of their theoretical work focuses on street crime, "hard" police tactics (e.g., stopping and searching people who are publicly drunk), and woman abuse in intimate relationships (DeKeseredy, Schwartz, Fagen, and Hall, 2006; Friedrichs, 2009). The main reason for this is that prior to the 1980s, most critical criminologists focused primarily on corporate and white-collar crime, as well as the influence of class and race/ethnic relations on definitions of crime and the administration of justice. Again, left realists, too, are concerned about these problems, but contend that ignoring crimes committed in urban streets by "the truly disadvantaged" (Wilson, 1987) and behind closed doors by patriarchal, abusive men enables right-wing politicians to manufacture ideological support for draconian criminal justice policies that harm people at the bottom of the socioeconomic ladder and that preclude the creation of society based on class, race/ethnic, and gender equality (Boehringer, Brown, Edgeworth, Hogg, and Ramsey, 1983; Taylor, 1992). Moreover, left realists claim that the left's ongoing neglect in taking working-class victimization seriously contributes to the right's hegemonic control over knowledge about crime and policing (DeKeseredy and Schwartz, 1991a). As US left realist Elliott Currie (1992) observes, ignoring predatory and domestic crimes in socially and economically excluded urban communities only serves to:

> help perpetuate an image of progressives as being both fuzzy-minded and, much worse, unconcerned about the realities of life for those ordinary Americans who are understandably frightened and enraged by the suffering and fear crimes brings to their communities and families.
>
> (p. 91)

Left realists point to the criminogenic consequences of broader social forces such as patriarchy and capitalism, but they also borrow from mainstream theoretical work done by strain theorists Merton (1938) and Cohen (1955). For example, early British left realist theorizing focused heavily on the concepts of relative deprivation and subculture. According to Lea and Young (1984, p. 88), it is

> poverty experienced as unfair (relative deprivation when compared to someone else) that creates discontent; and discontent where there is

no political solution leads to crime. The equation is simple: relative deprivation equals discontent: discontent plus lack of political solution equals crime.

Somewhat similar to what Albert Cohen (1955) argued, Lea and Young also contend that people lacking legitimate means of solving the problem of relative deprivation may come into contact with other frustrated, disenfranchised people and form subcultures, which, in turn, encourage and legitimate criminal behaviors (Young, 1999). Absent from this theory, however, is an attempt to address how criminogenic subcultural development in North America and other industrialized parts of the world is simultaneously shaped by the recent destructive consequences of free-market policies and marginalized men's attempts to live up to the principles of hegemonic masculinity. DeKeseredy and Schwartz's (in press) new left realist theory prioritizes these two variables and offers a more gendered understanding of the linkage between broader social forces and subcultural development.

Briefly, DeKeseredy and Schwartz (in press) assert that the harmful effects of "laissez-faire" economic policies informed by Friedman (1962) and others on the right have caused a relatively "new assault" on workers and have helped make North America "categorically unequal" (Massey, 2007), including corporations moving to developing countries to use cheap labor and take advantage of weak environmental and workplace safety laws (DeKeseredy and Schwartz, 2002; Wacquant, 2008). The main point is that they have excluded a substantial number of North Americans from the labor market, which challenges many men's masculine identity. A major source of many male youth's discontent is their unemployment and "material shortage" relative to the employment and "material abundance" of male members of other social-class groupings (Ellis and DeKeseredy, 1996). Many of these socially and economically excluded youths, regardless of whether they live in urban or rural communities, experience "status frustration" that puts them at great risk of teaming up with others to create a subculture that promotes, expresses, and validates masculinity through violent means (Cohen, 1955; DeKeseredy and Schwartz, 2005b; Hagedorn, 1988; Messerschmidt, 1993).

DeKeseredy and Schwartz (in press) further assert that in communities damaged by deindustrialization, the loss of family-owned farms, the closing of sawmills and coal mines, and so on, there is a greater proportion of all-male peer groups that promote violence against women. Men at the bottom of the socio-economic ladder flocking together with members of all-male sexist subcultures that perpetuate and legitimate woman abuse is not surprising, since they are more likely than their more affluent counterparts to adhere to the ideology of familial patriarchy (DeKeseredy et al., 2003; Smith, 1990). Arguably, such subcultures are likely to flourish in the near future because areas with high levels of poverty and unemployment are fertile breeding grounds for male-to-male and male-to-female violence (Currie, 2008a). This is not to say, however, that middle-class men and boys do not engage in violence. They certainly do, and there is a large empirical and theoretical literature on the strong correlation between patriarchal male peer support and various types of woman abuse in university/college dating, which involves, for the most part, middle- and upper-class young adults (DeKeseredy and Schwartz, 2009). Male peer support is the attachment to male peers and the resources they provide that perpetuate and legitimate woman abuse (DeKeseredy, 1990).

Thus far, this section has only touched on pieces of the complex theoretical background of left realism. For example, left realists also offer a timely, but not widely cited, theoretical model directing attention to the negative outcomes of criminalizing incivilities, such as public drunkenness and panhandling in urban communities (Kinsey, Lea, and Young, 1986). Moreover, left realists have created the "square" of crime that focuses simultaneously on the community, the state, the victim, and the offender (Young, 1992). Jennifer Gibbs (in press) also offers a left realist perspective on terrorism. However, similar to what Friedrichs (2009, p. 214) refers to as "traditional radical criminology," left realism has not addressed crimes committed by white middle-class youth, which is an issue of major concern for US left realist Elliott Currie (2004).

Based on in-depth interviews with young men and women, Currie fills a major gap in left realist theorizing by revealing that many of today's white middle-class youths are on a "road to whatever." "Whatever" is a word that many of his respondents and other teenagers use to describe how they felt before committing dangerous or self-destructive acts. It is, according to Currie, "an emotional place in which they no longer cared about what happened to them and that made trouble not only possible but likely" (Currie, 2004, p. 14). What motivates them to start and continue this journey? The conservative knee-jerk response to this question is leniency, inadequate discipline, the ethos of self-expression, and other symptoms of "liberalism." Currie shows that nothing could be further from the truth. Certainly, since the 1990s, lawmakers in the United States, Canada, and other advanced industrial nations have passed draconian legislation aimed at regulating youth deviance, and zero-tolerance policies are now common approaches to dealing with minor transgressions and incivilities in schools across North America and elsewhere (DeKeseredy, 2007).

Currie offers an empirically informed theory of juvenile troubles that emphasizes the role of modern social Darwinist culture. For example, he asserts that the "road to whatever" starts in youths' families, "which often embody the 'sink or swim' ethos of the larger culture – a neglectful and punitive individualism that sets adolescents up for feelings of failure, worthlessness, and heedlessness that can erode their capacity to care about themselves or others" (Currie, 2004, p. 14). Darwinism also guides techniques helping professionals and teachers to treat troubled middle-class teenagers, and statements made by Currie's interviewees show that "there is no help out there" for many delinquent youths raised in Darwinian households. In fact, teachers and therapists driven by Darwinian thought exacerbated the interviewees' problems.

While, for some people, left realism may be "half-forgotten," it is still very much at the forefront of many scholars' minds (DeKeseredy et al., 2006). Numerous criminologists continue to review (often inaccurately) this school of thought in undergraduate texts and in scholarly books and journals. That Roger Matthews' (2009) re-fashioned realism is published in the widely read and cited journal *Theoretical Criminology* is a strong indicator that left realism is "making a comeback." More evidence of the rebirth of left realism is the fact that the journal *Crime, Law and Social Change* has published a special issue on left realism, edited by Martin Schwartz and myself. Moreover, Matthews' (2009) call for linking theory, method, and intervention challenges the portrayal of left realism as "representing more of an ideological emphasis than a theory" (Schmalleger and Volk, 2005, p. 300). Such criticisms create an "us versus them" scenario in which conservative or mainstream criminologists are objective scientists pursuing the truth, while left realists and other critical criminologists, at best, only pay lip service to rigorous theoretical, empirical, and policy work (DeKeseredy and Dragiewicz, 2007).

Nevertheless, left realism, like any social scientific school of thought, has limitations. One, in particular, is the ongoing inattention given to female offending (DeKeseredy *et al.*, 2006). Women, too, suffer from relative deprivation, belong to subcultures, and are exposed to the same mass media and cultural influences promoting capitalist and individualist materialist acquisition, all of which should give them the motivation needed to commit street crimes and to obtain desired objects (DeKeseredy and Schwartz, 2005b). Yet, compared to men and boys, most females do not do this. Left realist theory is still weak on this case and could benefit by addressing the work of feminist scholars such as Chesney-Lind and Pasko (2004), Miller (2001), and Walklate (2004).

PEACEMAKING CRIMINOLOGY[11]

The United States is one of the most violent countries in the world. It is also the most punitive nation in the world. The US incarceration rate is over 700 per 100,000 population, and the United States is one of the only advanced industrial countries that still uses the death penalty (Currie, 2008a). US citizens are now imprisoned four times more than in the early 1970s (Foster and Hagen, 2007; Western, Pattillo, and Weiman, 2004), and this "mass incarceration" or "new penalism" is racialized (Chesney-Lind, 2007; DeKeseredy, 2009a). About one out of every three African-American men between the ages of 20 and 29 are under some type of correctional supervision, while Latinos stand a 17 percent chance of being incarcerated (Mauer, 2005).

There is much more evidence showing that the United States has shifted from a "welfare state" to a "penal state" (Wacquant, 2001). Yet, capital punishment, long-term prison sentences, and other harsh sanctions are not making US streets, homes, and intimate relationships safer. In fact, extreme harshness is a conservative social experiment that has clearly failed (Reiman and Leighton, 2010). In response to this ongoing crisis, many criminologists contend that it is now time for politicians, criminal justice officials, and members of the general public to recognize that the United States and other very punitive countries (e.g., Russian Federation) are going about things the wrong way. However, there are many conflicting answers to the question, "What is to be done about crime and its control?"

Some people, including conservative politicians, call for a criminal justice system that is even more punitive than the current one (DeKeseredy, 2009a). One benefit of claiming that the system is not harsh enough is that no matter how harsh it becomes, there is no way of proving that it isn't harsh "enough" (DeKeseredy and Schwartz, 1996). If getting harsher does not seem to have any important effect on crime, there is always room for people to assert that we need to get harsher still. Other people, however, contend that radical individual, structural, and cultural changes constitute the solution to crime problems. Among this group are peacemaking criminologists such as Harold Pepinsky and Richard Quinney (1991). Peacemaking criminologists see crime as only one of many different types of violence – such as war, racism, and sexism – that contribute to human suffering (Thomas and O'Maolchatha, 1989).

In the early 1990s, British criminologist Paul Rock (1992) stated that "one might remark that criminology undergoes a scientific revolution *every* time Jock Young changes his mind" (p. x; emphasis in original). Across the Atlantic Ocean, in the United States, a similar observation was recently made about another prominent critical criminologist. According to Lilly *et al.* (2007, pp. 179–180), "Perhaps nothing exemplifies the way in which the context of the times conditions the development of criminological theory so clearly in the evolution in the thinking of Quinney," especially as he moved into peacemaking criminology. Quinney and other peacemaking criminologists are informed by anarchism, humanism, Christian socialism, liberation theology, Eastern meditative thought, penal abolitionism, feminism, and Marxism.[12] According to Pepinsky (2008, p. 190), "part of the art and science of peacemaking is to work out when and how to draw a balance between offering empathy and resisting abuse and violence." Peacemaking also includes the following basic principles, as outlined by Quinney (1991):

- Crime is suffering, and crime can only be eliminated by ending suffering.
- Crime and suffering can only be ended through the achievement of peace.
- Human transformation will achieve peace and justice.
- Human transformation will occur if we change our social, economic, and political structure.

For peacemaking criminologists, the current criminal justice system is a failure because it is rooted in the very problem it is ostensibly designed to eliminate – violence. A "war on crime," a "war on drugs," and all of the other "wars" we fight are based on the presumption that we can "stamp out," "eradicate," "push back," or otherwise do something violent to crime. Thus, for example, many people presume that crime can be stopped by enacting even harsher sanctions, even for relatively minor incivilities (Kelling and Coles, 1997). When this does not work, we increase penalties further. And then more again. And then still more again (DeKeseredy and Schwartz, 1996). Peacemaking criminologists do not believe that we can end violence through violence; such tactics only lead to violent reactions to our own violence (Pepinksy, 2008).

Peacemaking criminology shares some ideas with other progressive criminological perspectives, including anarchic or abolitionist criminology and restorative justice (de Haan, 2009; Fuller and Wozniak, 2006). However, the restorative justice movement is also embraced by some mainstream criminologists and has been co-opted by the criminal justice system (Friedrichs, 2009). Here, following Ptacek (2010a), restorative justice is defined as an approach that seeks "to decrease the role of the state in responding to crime and increase the involvement of personal, familial, and community networks in repairing the harm caused by crime" (p. ix). On the other hand, abolitionism can in no way be considered conservative, given that it calls for the total elimination of prisons, the death penalty, and solitary confinement, as well as a formal government and its laws (de Hann, 2009; Morris, 1995; Friedrichs, 2009).

What stands peacemaking criminologists apart from others is that they want to "make peace on crime." They call for a nonviolent criminology, one that simultaneously rejects repressive measures (e.g., prisons) and embraces human, progressive, community-based strategies such as mediation, reconciliation, alternative dispute resolution, and other nonpenal means of making our society safer (DeKeseredy and Schwartz, 1996). The success of such strategies and other less punitive community-based initiatives support the argument put forth nearly 30 years ago by Stanley Cohen (1985, p. 131):

> It still makes sense to say that mutual aid, good neighborliness and real community are preferable to the solutions of bureaucracies, professionals and the centralized state.... [I]t should not be impossible to imagine a way of stopping the relentless categorization of deviants.

It is not surprising that conservatives see peacemaking criminology as a "heretical challenge" to their draconian crime control strategies (Friedrichs, 2009). Others, including some who are critical criminologists, simply label peacemaking as utopian (Gibbons, 1994). Again, it has been co-opted by the criminal justice system. For example, judges who feel that probation is not a strong enough sanction might "sentence" a youth to restitution, community service, and charitable donations. Across Canada, the United States, and other countries juvenile court judges do this mainly with the idea that such moves are more a punishment than regular probation (Ptacek, 2010b). The youths themselves figure out quickly that this is a form of punishment, and the probation officers send out that message easily enough. In such an environment, some restitution might be paid and some beer cans picked up on a road outside of town, but no lessons are being learned either by the offenders or by the community (DeKeseredy and Schwartz, 1996).

Restorative practices, such as some of those advanced by peacemaking criminologists, are now found in over 80 countries (Porter, 2005), and the United Nations has adopted the basic principles of restorative justice and encourages countries to implement them (Parker, 2007; Van Ness, 2002). However, many feminists doubt that certain peacemaking responses are effective solutions to male violence against women. Such skepticism is well-founded, because some women abused by male intimates are also harmed during the process of court mediation (Ptacek, 2010b). This is what happened to 34 abused Nova Scotia women:

> Abused women reported intimidation and revictimization in mediation regardless of the form of abuse: physical, sexual, emotional, psychological, or financial. Women reported that their mediator or conciliator minimized emotional, psychological, or financial abuse, or simply did not recognize certain behaviors as abusive. When women brought up the fact that their ex-partner was harassing, stalking, or otherwise continuing to abuse them during the mediation, their mediators did not terminate mediation.
>
> (Rubin, 2000, p. 8)

Although there is much controversy among feminists about peacemaking criminology and violence against women,[13] some left realists claim that a program of reconciliation, re-education, and mutual aid by a caring community would offer the greatest hope of ending many other behaviors that induce a fearful state in wide numbers of women, such as various forms of sexual harassment in public places. Expanding the net of social control could bring in male perpetrators to begin a process of stopping their harassment of women, which, in the long run, would do more to demarginalize women than many other criminology proposals (DeKeseredy and Schwartz, 1991b). Of course, careful attention needs to be paid to the fact that peacemaking solutions are only useful as part of a package that includes structural change in society, or such solutions may render conflict as individual and deny structure (Selva and Bohm, 1987).

In sum, even if peacemaking criminologists' strategies for making the world peaceful stand little, if any, chance of being implemented under the current patriarchal capitalist social order, their work can constantly alert criminologists, politicians, the media, and the general public that there are alternatives to ceaseless and counterproductive wars on crime (DeKeseredy and Schwartz, 1996; Friedrichs, 2009). They can take the first steps toward developing the social changes and interconnections between people that peacemaking criminologists feel are essential to reducing crime. As Martin Schwartz (1991) points out in his evaluation of peacemaking criminology, at the very least this perspective can help us think through our "facile acceptance of violence against others" (p. 123).

POSTMODERN CRIMINOLOGY[14]

With origins mainly in France and Germany, postmodern thought has had a major impact on many academics, especially those based in university English departments and who specialize in literary criticism (Curran and Renzetti, 2001). However, it was not until the late 1980s that postmodernism began to influence a number of critical criminologists (Henry and Milovanovic, 2005).[15] Still, a cautionary note is required here. As Friedrichs (2009, p. 213) observes, "postmodern thought itself is by no means necessarily linked with a progressive agenda; on the contrary, much postmodernist thought is viewed as either consciously apolitical or inherently conservative and reactionary."

What is postmodern criminology? Briefly answering this question is a major challenge because there are numerous postmodern perspectives (Schwartz and Friedrichs, 1994). Further, postmodern theory is so hard to grasp – even for those who have deeply studied the issues involved – that only a superficial overview will be offered here. It is, to say the least, extremely difficult, if not impossible, to adequately explain postmodernism in a short section of a book like this. Thus, following Friedrichs (2009), postmodern criminology can best be described here as "a loose collection of themes and tendencies" (p. 213).

One of postmodernism's central ideas is deep skepticism about knowledge claims. Postmodernists reject claims of objectivity and challenge the modernist notion that we can harness science and logic, discover truth, and then put that truth to work to solve problems like crime (DeKeseredy and Schwartz, 1996). For postmodernists, "truth" is a social construction and a form of domination because it represents a way of looking at things that is imposed by those with more power (Curran and Renzetti, 2001; Wonders, 1999). Reality is not easily knowable, but rather is very complex, hard to read, and contradictory.

Postmodernists do not believe that *any* knowledge is knowable. They think that *any* truth claims are a form of tyranny and reject any claims by anyone who purports to know what is right. If truth is unknowable (Henry and Milovanovic, 2005), then our quest for knowledge must come from an understanding that everything is relative or related to everything else (Schwartz and Friedrichs, 1994). We need to be careful that we are not imposing our values (truth) on other people, which is a key issue for many postmodernists. Whereas progressives in general always try to speak for oppressed social groups, postmodernists warn about trying to speak for these people, rather than allowing them to speak for themselves (Denzin, 1990).

Some theorists argue that postmodern criminology is perhaps best understood in terms of what it opposes (Ferrell, 1998; Lilly *et al.*, 2007). Not surprisingly, postmodernism rejects positivism and the potential of collective social action to change society (Friedrichs, 2009). Postmodernism also, as cultural criminologist Jeff Ferrell (1998) once argued, opposes "the intellectual and legal machinery of modernism" and the "forms of legality, illegality, and crime that criminology conventionally investigates" (p. 63). Postmodernists are also against any broad, general theory of anything, at best suggesting that local people everywhere need to develop their own definitions of their experiences and need to work out their own methods of resistance to oppression (DeKeseredy and Schwartz, 1996).

Another one of postmodernist criminology's central ideas is that written or spoken language always plays a major role in the reality we construct and live (Arrigo, 2003). Hence, postmodernists "deconstruct" the meanings and social processes that we connect to crime and criminal justice (Curran and Renzetti, 2001; Friedrichs, 2009). As postmodern criminologist Bruce Arrigo (2003) puts it:

Deconstruction or "trashing" entails a careful reading and de-coding of a text (written or spoken). The purpose of deconstructing the text is to unveil the implicit assumptions and hidden values (i.e., often inconsistent, contradictory beliefs about social phenomena) embedded within a particular narrative. Deconstruction shows us how certain truth claims are privileged within a given story, while certain others are disguised or dismissed altogether. Because deconstruction focuses on the actual words people use to convey their thoughts, it attempts to uncover the unconscious intent behind the grammar people employ when writing or speaking. Thus, language or entire systems of communication are put under the microscope for closer inspection. In a sense, then, trashing a text entails reading between the lines to ascertain meanings (i.e., ideology) given preferred status in a particular language system.

(p. 48)

What has been described so far is quite abstract. Postmodernists must contend with accusations that they are irrelevant theorists who are more concerned with making petty academic points in obscure terms than they are with effecting serious change in the world (Schwartz and Friedrichs, 1994). Related to this point is that postmodernists have also been accused of being apolitical or being politically neutral (Curran and Renzetti, 2001; Dews, 1987; Melichar, 1990), which is also why much postmodernist work is deemed to be inherently conservative (Friedrichs, 2009). Of course, the problem is that there are so many versions of postmodernism in the social sciences that virtually any broad claims do not encompass everyone working within the tradition (Rosenau, 1992). Therefore, what Curran and Renzetti (2001) stated in their review of postmodern criminology is applicable here: "No doubt, many criminologists who call themselves postmodernists will object to our characterization of it here" (p. 205).

No critical criminology text that focuses on postmodern criminology is complete without a summary of "constitutive criminology," a school of thought developed by Stuart Henry and Dragan Milovanovic (1993, 2003). What is particularly interesting is that they integrate postmodernism into a more traditional criminological framework, with the goal of working on the production of meaning in the area of crime. They argue that such meaning is "co-produced" by those who engage in crime, those who try to control it, and those who study it.

Henry and Milovanovic would agree with much of the left realist and feminist analyses and strongly approve of peacemaking criminology's rejection of the use of state violence to overcome individual violence. However, they would define crime as the power to create pain or harm in any context, so that:

> law is not just a definer of crime, it is also a maker of crime. This is because it conceals some people's harms by reflecting power relations, and it manifests crime through its own exercise of power over others, especially those whose own activities have not been to deny others their own expression, such as is the case of consensual "crime," or crimes without victims.
>
> (Henry and Milovanovic, 1993, p. 12)

Thus, Henry and Milovanovic call for a short-term, "social judo" response to violence, whereby, instead of engaging in violence with the government, those who are oppressed by it must learn to bend or channel others' exercise of power over them into the exercise of power over others. The goal is

> a minimal use of energy toward redirecting the considerable power of those seeking to exercise power over us, such that they are made abundantly aware that the more energy they expend in harming us the more that energy converts into constraining them, limiting their further ability to harm us. This is the challenge of a transformative political agenda.
>
> (Henry and Milovanovic, 1993, p. 12)

This analysis is similar to the arguments of feminist postmodernism generally (DeKeseredy and Schwartz, 1996), which has strongly opposed romantic theorists who have championed their identification with oppressed groups. They argue that gathering strength by such identification is impossible. A better goal would be resisting "group identities that have been formed in hierarchical contexts [that] will only reproduce those hierarchical relationships (or, at best, create new ones)" (Grant, 1993, p. 137).

CULTURAL CRIMINOLOGY

Cultural criminology is one of the newest directions in critical criminology and was born in the mid-1990s (Ferrell, 1994, 1995; Ferrell and Sanders, 1995). This contemporary critical criminological school of thought is also a prime example of intellectual and political cross-fertilization, because its pioneers (e.g., Jeff Ferrell, Mike Presdee, Keith Hayward, and Jock Young) are based in the United States and the United Kingdom. There are, of course, cultural criminologists in other parts of the world, including Canada, where Ryerson University professor Stephen Muzzatti has made several important contributions to the field.[16] Sadly, one of cultural criminology's founders – Mike Presdee – passed away in July 2009.[17] In Box 2.1, Jock Young (2009, pp. 1–2) describes Presdee's contributions to the growth of cultural criminology. Presdee's work will always be remembered, and the ASC's DCC honored him posthumously by awarding him the DCC Lifetime Achievement Award in 2009.

Box 2.1 Mike Presdee: Perceptive Sociologist Who Played a
Key Role in the Growth of Cultural Criminology

Mike Presdee, who has died of cancer aged 64, was a sociologist of international acclaim and great personal magnetism. His work focused on the sociology of youth and cultural criminology. He was fascinated by the way in which young people can be criminalized and controlled, and of youth being seen as a problem, rather than young people being the locus of the problems of the system. In later life, he attempted to understand and explain New Labour's neurotic obsession with antisocial behavior.

Cultural criminology was made for Mike and he was one of its chief architects. He was part of a generation of British criminologists entering academia during the post-1960s era of expanded university provision, who no longer looked down the class structure from a position of privilege, gazing with interest, sometimes charity, but always social distance.

Rather, they spoke for those low in the social structure, and were aware not only of the background factors of social action but the foreground rush of consciousness which gives it life and meaning.

Where traditional criminology mistakes textual dullness and robot-like social actors for objectivity, cultural criminology zooms in on the phenomenal experience of crime, victimization and punishment, stressing anger, humiliation, exuberance, excitement, and fear. It reveals the energy of everyday life, whether in the transgressive breaking of rules or in the repressive nature of conformity and boredom.

Mike's *Cultural Criminology and the Carnival of Crime* (2000) epitomized this approach. A firecracker of a book, it focuses on everything from joyriding to hate crimes, from the criminalization of raves to sadomasochism, it explores notions of transgression and resistance. It introduces the work of Mikhail Bakhtin, Gilles Deleuze and Theodor Reik, and is inspired by the earlier work of Jack Katz, Dick Hebdige, and Jeff Ferrell. It is one of the best introductions to cultural criminology and holds students spellbound.

Near the end of the book's acknowledgments, he apologized to his friends for enjoying life too much and to his employers for seeming to enjoy work too little. And that was it: Mike was a bon vivant, an intellectual enthusiast, a committed Marxist, a proud father, an inspired writer, a bit of an agitator – a wonderful man.

Cultural criminology has roots in the writings of US labeling theorists (e.g., Becker, 1973; Lemert, 1951), British youth cultural and subcultural theorists (e.g., Hall, Critcher, Jefferson, Clarke, and Roberts, 1978; Willis, 1977), moral panic theorists (e.g., Cohen, 1980; Young, 1971), and, of course, the "new criminologists" of the 1970s, such as Taylor, Walton, and Young (1973). Social constructionism, postmodern critical theory, and media/content analysis also heavily inform cultural criminology (Hayward, 2007; Hayward and Young,

2004; Muzzatti, 2006). As described by Jeff Ferrell (2003, p. 71), cultural criminology:

> critically investigates the ways in which the dynamics of media and popular culture, the lives and activities of criminals, and the operations of social control and criminal justice come together in everyday life. Cultural criminologists emphasize the role of image, style, and symbolic meaning among criminals and their subcultures, in the mass media's representation of crime and criminal justice, and in public conflicts over crime and crime control.

Like some feminist analyses (e.g., Chesney-Lind and Irwin, 2008), the role of media-generated moral panics is central to cultural criminologists' theoretical work. For example, in the United States and Canada, there is an important battle being waged over the nature of women's violence and aggression (DeKeseredy and Dragiewicz, 2007; Schwartz and DeKeseredy, 1993). Similarly, there is, in typical US style, a "war on girls" (DeKeseredy, in press a). Some well-known and widely used weapons in this war are "condemnatory media images" of teenage girls, such as those involving relational aggression in Hollywood movies like *Mean Girls* (Chesney-Lind and Irwin, 2008; Schissel, 1997). Cultural criminologists, among others, point out that such films, statistically rare cases of brutal female violence reported by the media, and untrue claims of a major surge in female youth violence like that offered in James Garbarino's (2006) controversial trade book, *See Jane Hit*, fuel moral panics about girls deemed to be in conflict with the law or who use various means of rebelling against patriarchal dominance in schools, dance halls, at home, and elsewhere.

The concept of the moral panic was developed by Stanley Cohen (1980) to describe a situation in which a condition, episode, person, or a group of persons come to be defined as a threat to society. The objects of moral panics are usually people. Certainly, the media, together with some social scientists, lawyers, agents of social control, and other "experts," have jumped on the bandwagon to transform girls who violate a myriad of patriarchal gender norms in the United States, Canada, and other parts of the world into folk devils. A folk devil is "a socially constructed, stereotypical carrier of significant social harm" (Ellis, 1987, p. 199). As vividly pointed out by scholars who analyze the media with a gendered lens, many girls are labeled as being made up of "sugar and spice and everything evil" (Schissel, 1997, p. 51).

As stated above, cultural criminology also draws heavily from important studies on youth culture and subcultures, and offers "thick" descriptions of people who live at the edge of conventional society (e.g., drug users, skydivers, and graffiti artists) (Ferrell, Hayward, and Young, 2008; Friedrichs, 2009). However, the use of the concept "culture" is subject to criticism. For instance, it is said that cultural criminologists' definition of culture is more political than analytical (Lilly *et al.*, 2007; O'Brien, 2005). This is, though, a rather old critique and claims of subjectivity or "blatant violations" of traditional scientific modes of inquiry have been directed at critical criminologists and other progressive scholars for decades (Muzzatti, 2006). Following in the footsteps of critics of 1960s and early 1970s labeling theory, others claim that cultural criminology's analyses of high-profile crime, social deviants, and moral panics is similar to a criminology of "nuts, sluts, and perverts" and "the exotic, the erotic and the neurotic" (Adler and Adler, 2003; Liazos, 1972). Muzzatti (2006, p. 75) responds to such criticism by stating:

> These critiques incorrectly equate style with a lack of substance. Because the mediated reality of crime is fundamentally a political endeavor, cultural criminology's engagement with these actors, texts and processes can be seen as a retaliatory strike in the culture wars. Cultural criminology offers an avenue for intellectual resistance and self-defense against conventional constructions of crime and prescriptions for control.

Another frequent criticism of cultural criminology is that it "overemphasizes" with the subcultures and other "outlaws" and thus lacks a solid appreciation of the legitimate concerns of those responsible for responding and preventing their activities, such as the police, teachers, and the like (Friedrichs, 2009). Nevertheless, cultural criminology is "here to stay," and it is attracting an international cadre of dedicated scholars (DeKeseredy and Perry,

2006b). The launch of relatively new journals such as *Crime, Media, Culture*, and special editions of established journals such as *Theoretical Criminology*, as well as the publication of some widely read and cited books (e.g., Ferrell *et al.*, 2008) attest to this emerging orientation (Muzzatti, 2006).

CONVICT CRIMINOLOGY

Prisoners and ex-convicts have long been the subject of criminological inquiry. However, the bulk of the empirical and theoretical work on these groups is done by criminologists who have had little contact with the criminal justice system (Ross and Richards, 2003). There is also another group of criminologists, such as those who specialize in the psychology of criminal conduct (e.g., Andrews and Bonta, 2006), who routinely enter correctional institutions only to subject prisoners to a battery of problematic psychological tests that end up supporting their claim that crime is primarily a property of the individual (Davidson and Chesney-Lind, 2009). Such work fails to address the real experiences of convicts and ex-convicts (Friedrichs, 2009), which is one of the key reasons for the birth of convict criminology.

"Primarily an American contribution" (Lilly *et al.*, 2007, p. 203), convict criminology formally started at the 1997 ASC meeting and includes academic criminologists who have served time in correctional facilities, as well as some progressive scholars who have not been officially designated as criminal or deviant. In the words of Ross and Richards (2003, p. 6):

> This is a "new criminology" (I. Taylor, Walton, and Young, 1973) led by ex-convicts who are now academic faculty. These men and women, who have worn both prison uniforms and academic regalia, served years behind prison walls, and now as academics, are the primary architects of the movement. The convict scholars do what most previous writers could not: merge their past with their present and provide a provocative approach to the academic study of criminology, criminal justice, and corrections. These authors, as a collective, are the future of a realistic paradigm that promises to challenge the conventional research findings of the past.

Not to be confused with penal abolitionism, which calls for abolishing prisons, the death penalty, and solitary confinement (Lilly *et al.*, 2007; Morris, 1995), convict criminology involves the use of ethnographic studies of the prison experience to "tell it like it is" (Ross and Richards, 2003, p. 9). Given their first-hand experiences with penal institutions, convict criminologists are certainly highly qualified experts in their fields and offer unique "inside perspectives" based on rigorous, thoughtful studies of prison life. Further, these critical scholars are among a large group of progressives that point to the destructive nature of prisons and their inability to promote peace, reduce crime, and foster social justice. As Ross and Richards (2003, p. 3) observe, "One cursory look at the gun towers, walls, and razor wire is evidence that prisons were built to warehouse and punish and not to rehabilitate."

Nearly 20 years ago, David Friedrichs (1991) claimed that it is rather premature to consider peacemaking criminologists' contributions a "school of thought." Perhaps the same assertion can be applied to convict criminology. As Alan Mobley (2003, p. 223) puts it, "Criminology is a curious business and it is not clear where, or if, the convict criminologist fits in." Convict criminology is vibrant and the ASC meetings routinely feature dynamic sessions on this new variant of critical criminology. Nevertheless, some critics wonder whether it is doing anything novel except for the fact that a sizeable portion of convict criminologists publicly reveal their status as "ex-cons." Moreover, convict criminologists are somewhat stigmatized for not publishing in mainstream journals, and, of course, the claim of being too subjective is frequently made (Lilly *et al.*, 2007).

What critics are missing, however, is that convict criminologists are opposed to mainstream or "managerial criminology," which is why they publish in alternative venues. The same can be said about many proponents of other new directions in critical criminology. Also, as stated earlier in this book and elsewhere, there is no such thing as value-free research, and every study, theory, or policy is informed by politics. In addition, since convict criminology is a relatively new school of thought, it is destined to generate new ways of thinking critically about crime, law, and social control. Hopefully, what Ross and

Richards (2003) stated at the start of this century will come true: "We predict that over time, this new school of convict criminology will provide the public with a more realistic understanding of crime, criminal justice, and corrections that is based on experience and cutting-edge research" (p. 13).

SUMMARY[18]

Theory construction and testing occur every day. Nevertheless, some of the most popular journals in the field, such as *Criminology*, only pay lip service to new directions in critical criminology, as well as other theories, and are heavily invested in publishing variants of "so what? criminology" characterized by impenetrable statistical analyses (Currie, 2007). Today, especially in the United States, being labeled a theorist or referring to oneself as such results in marginalization and difficulties landing a tenure-track position at a prestigious university or college. On the other hand, those deemed as "good researchers" are more likely to be "in with the in crowd" and stand a much better chance of getting an academic post at a large doctoral institution.

Criminology is fragmented and academic criminology is under siege (DeKeseredy and Schwartz, in press). Moreover, due in large part to the devastating effects of free-market economic policies, universities and colleges are increasingly demanding that faculty obtain more external funds. Doing this is not an easy task for progressive scholars with a vested interest in theory construction. For example, most government agencies that fund criminological work have relatively little money to begin with, and those in charge of them call for research that evaluates the efficiency of mainstream policies, laws, and practices (Savelsberg, King, and Cleveland, 2002; Walters, 2003). Consequently, as Matthews (2009, p. 341) notes, "academic criminology appears to be becoming more marginalized and irrelevant."

There is much public support for the marginalization and gutting of the humanities and social sciences, which is one of the key reasons why conservative politicians get elected. Further, many people view the theoretical work done by scholars in these fields as simply academic products of "impractical mental gymnastics" or "fanciful ideas that have little to do with what truly motivates people" (Akers, 1997, p. 1). However, let us return to Kurt Lewin's (1951) claim about the practicality of theory. Critical criminologists agree with him and assert that one of the key reasons for why much criminological work is not policy relevant is that much of it is a-theoretical (Matthews, 2009). As is the case with illnesses, such as AIDS, prior to finding solutions to crime and injustice, we must first identify the causes, and critical criminologists have long argued for linking theory to practice (Young, 1992).

The main objective of this chapter was to introduce some of the most important current trends in critical criminology. All of them have shown themselves to be important alternatives to traditional criminological theory and more critical perspectives are likely to emerge in the near future. As stated above, although the schools of thought reviewed here were presented in a particular order, all of them are equally important and each one has strengths and limitations. There is no such thing as a perfect theory of crime or social control (Curran and Renzetti, 2001).

In late 1980s and early 1990s, the criminological world saw the development of four new directions in critical criminology: feminism, left realism, peacemaking, and postmodernism. In response to the emergence of these progressive perspectives, Schwartz (1991) stated that critical criminology "is infused with more energy and exciting alternatives than at any point in the past 20 years" and that "there are so many more avenues and ideas to develop" (p. 123). The same can be said today. That more new ways of thinking critically about crime have been developed since Schwartz made his observation offers some support for the hypothesis that "the impact of critical criminology will increase exponentially in the years ahead, perhaps at some point even coming to overshadow mainstream forms of analysis" (Friedrichs, 2009, p. 217). Will such a transition actually occur? This is an empirical question that can only be answered empirically. Yet, given the exciting developments reviewed here and elsewhere, the future looks promising.

3

CONTEMPORARY CRITICAL CRIMINOLOGICAL RESEARCH

It is not the method that designates an approach as critical: critical researchers use a diverse range of methods, and methods are not "inherently positivist, phenomenological or critical" (Harvey, 1990, p. 1). Critical research is shaped "at the level of methodology" (Harvey, 1990, p. 201). Some areas of critical criminology do have an orientation towards a particular method or methods, with a strong tendency towards qualitative approaches such as participant observation or in-depth interviews. However, debates about the relative merits of qualitative or quantitative research commonly express epistemological or methodological differences. At the level of methods, multi-methods approaches (methodological triangulation) commonly employ both qualitative and quantitative methods that have different strengths. For critical criminology, as for other traditions, the appropriate method depends on the research objectives.

(Stubbs, 2008, p. 13)

Critical criminologists examine a myriad of social problems, ranging from violence against women, to predatory street crime, to state or government crime. They also study timely and important issues outside the realm of criminology as it is commonly known. For example, US critical criminologist Raymond

Michalowski and his intimate partner anthropologist Jill Dubisch (2001) conducted an ethnographic study of a "secular pilgrimage" involving a motorcycle journey from southern California to the Vietnam War Memorial in Washington, DC. Consisting of Vietnam veterans, Michalowski and Dubisch joined this "run for the wall" in their hometown of Flagstaff, Arizona and ended up involved in a study that describes, in their words, "a journey that is both a physical passage through the nation and a spiritual and emotional journey toward healing and understanding" (p. ix).

Victoria Pitts-Taylor is another critical criminologist who "wears two hats." In addition to co-developing and testing a feminist routine activities theory of campus sexual assault (see Schwartz and Pitts, 1995), she does in-depth qualitative research on the experience, meanings, and motivations for cosmetic surgeries (Pitts-Taylor, 2007). Joseph Donnermeyer is one more prime example of a prominent critical criminologist who can balance more than one research project at the same time. Widely recognized as a pioneer in rural criminology, Donnermeyer also conducts studies of old order Amish social life in both Canada and the United States.[1] Cultural criminologists, too, are well known for doing empirical work outside the realm of conventional criminology. Consider Jeff Ferrell's (2006) ethnographic project on "dumpster diving" and studies of "edgework,"[2] such as advanced sky diving (Ferrell, Hayward, and Young, 2008; Lyng, 1990, 2005).

Many more examples of non-criminological research done by critical criminologists could easily be provided, such as Canadian scholar Stephen Muzzatti's (2005) analysis of mass media coverage of the outbreak of Severe Acute Respiratory Syndrome (SARS) in the spring of 2003. The key point here is that critical criminology is much more than a theoretical and/or political enterprise. It also entails "cutting edge" research on crimes at the top, crimes at the bottom, societal reactions to these harms, and how crime, law, and social control are influenced by broader social, political, cultural, and economic forces. The main objective of this chapter is to provide some major examples of recent critical criminological empirical contributions. It must be emphasized, though, that the studies reviewed in this chapter should not be considered superior to those not examined. Certainly, critical criminologists have attended to a legion of substantive topics and thus it is impossible to do them all justice in a short chapter or book.

INTERPERSONAL VIOLENCE[3]

It may seem counterintuitive to state that interpersonal violence is a new area of critical criminological inquiry. Still, until relatively recently such crime was not extensively examined by the discipline as a whole (DeKeseredy and Perry, 2006b). Some salient exceptions are studies of woman abuse done by feminists, left realists, and masculinities scholars. Masculinities and left realist research also focuses heavily on predatory street crimes (Friedrichs, 2009). Moreover, some of the methods used in these progressive studies are similar to those employed by mainstream scholars. One example is the victimization survey, a method commonly utilized to uncover "the dark figure of crime" or crimes not reported to the police. The self-report survey helps achieve the same goal; however, the former asks people about crimes committed against them, while the latter asks respondents to report the crimes they committed. What makes the mainstream use of such surveys distinct from how critical criminologists, such as left realists, use them is that conventional survey researchers focus primarily on individual characteristics, "rational calculations and routine activities, situational factors, and the more immediate environment" (Friedrichs, 2009, p. 216). Some of these factors are also addressed by surveys administered by progressive scholars, but there is a very strong emphasis on gleaning data on the influence of macro-level forces, such as the role of the ideology of familial patriarchy.

Even so, some determinants of central concern to critical criminologists have received more attention than others. For example, the ways in which race and class inequalities shape women's victimization in public and private places warrants much more scrutiny. Feminist scholar Jody Miller (2008) recently answered this call and studied gendered violence experienced by African-American girls in poor St. Louis neighborhoods. Miller conducted in-depth, semi-structured interviews with young African-American women and men, as well as surveys with them. Information on the characteristics of the participants' neighborhoods was also gathered. This project makes many important contributions, including being attentive to the victimization experiences of urban minority youth. Historically, criminologists mainly focused on minority youth in conflict with the law, such as street gang members, drug dealers, and so on. Miller (2008, p. 11) points out that:

> This is exacerbated by a general bias within American culture to assign greater importance to the victimization of whites than people of color and to take race into account when evaluating the seriousness of violence against women and the presumed culpability of its victims.

Miller's data also provide further evidence that the abuse of women is fostered by male peer support. Although the bulk of studies on the relationship between male peer support and woman abuse have been done on college campuses dominated by people of European descent, Miller's study supports what Lee Bowker (1983) said more than 30 years ago about all-male patriarchal subcultures of violence:

> This is not a subculture that is confined to a single class, religion, occupational grouping, or race. It is spread throughout all parts of society. Men are socialized by other subculture members to accept common definitions of the situation, norms, values, and beliefs about male dominance and the necessity of keeping their wives in line. These violence-supporting social relations may occur at any time and in any place.

(pp. 135–136)

Race, gender, and inner-city violence are key concerns for Nikki Jones (2010), who also conducted a study of African-American girls. Done in Philadelphia, this ethnographic project demonstrates how these girls manage the threat of daily interpersonal and gendered violence (e.g., sexual violence) in their neighborhoods. Like Miller (2008), Jones used multiple methods, including participant observation, direct observation, and informal interviews with girls who had voluntarily enrolled in a city hospital-based violence reduction project. Jones also participated in long conversations with the grandmothers, mothers, sisters, brothers, cousins, and friends of the young people in her study. Similar to Miller (2008), Jones (2010) does not pathologize her respondents of color. Rather, her work shows, contrary to the popular racist belief, that inner-city African-American girls are "resourceful, normal women" who are trying to negotiate and cope with brutal socioeconomic conditions in their communities.

As stated in Chapter 1, critical criminologists have not given much attention to crime and social control in rural communities, but we are now seeing an emergence of critical research on drug use, woman abuse, racism, and other social problems that plague rural areas in Canada, the United States, Australia, and elsewhere. Collectively, the rural studies cited in Chapter 1 show that rural communities are not less criminogenic than urban areas, a discovery that challenges conventional wisdom. In fact, rural rates may be higher than urban rates in particular types of rural places and for specific kinds of crime (Jobes, Barclay, Weinand, and Donnermeyer, 2004). Note that the official rate of violence for most rural counties in the United States exceeds that for several dozen metropolitan areas, based on the Federal Bureau of Investigation's (FBI) *Uniform Crime Reports* (Donnermeyer, 2007). North of the US border, in Canada, the rate of homicide in rural areas (2.5 per 100,000) is higher than the rate for large urban areas (2.0) and the rate for small urban communities (1.7), and this pattern held constant over a 10-year period (Statistics Canada, 2007a). Evidence also suggests that rural women are at greater risk of being sexually assaulted during and after separation/divorce than their urban counterparts (DeKeseredy and Schwartz, 2009). Indeed, critical criminologists are part of a cadre that alerts us to the fact that "[R]urality does not imply the sociological equivalent of immunity from crime" (Donnermeyer, Jobes, and Barclay, 2006, p. 205).

Structured social inequality is one of the key determinants of rural crime (Donnermeyer and DeKeseredy, 2008). Qualitative studies done in rural Appalachian sections of the United States by DeKeseredy, Schwartz, Fagen, and Hall (2006), Grant (2008), and Websdale (1998) show that woman abuse, alcoholism, and drug addiction are strongly associated with poverty, unemployment, and patriarchal practices and discourses. Similarly, societal reactions to these problems, such as policing, are also influenced by a larger set of economic, political, and social factors (Donnermeyer, DeKeseredy, and Dragiewicz, in press). As Grant (2008, p. 22) observes, "rural areas are often neglected in the creation of national political agenda or plans for reform and change."

Such neglect is also evident at the local level and is often linked to attempts to maintain inequality and oppression. DeKeseredy and Schwartz (2009) found that many rural Ohio men who abuse their ex-partners can rely on their male friends and neighbors, including those who are police officers, to support a violent patriarchal status quo even while they count on these same people to help prevent public crimes such as vandalism. Furthermore, in rural sections of Ohio and other states such as Kentucky, there is widespread acceptance of woman abuse and community norms prohibiting victims from publicly revealing their experiences and from seeking social support (DeKeseredy *et al.*, 2007). Rural women with addiction problems encounter similar processes of informal social control and hence spend long periods of time suffering in silence (Grant, 2008).

Masculinities researchers are another group of progressive scholars who open up new avenues of inquiry, one of which is the relationship between gender, the body, and violent crime. As Messerschmidt (2004, p. 19) notes:

> Feminists and profeminist criminologists historically have neglected how social action, lived experience, and crime are embodied. Not only have feminist and profeminist criminologists concentrated on gender differences in crime – thereby ignoring possible gender similarities in crime – they have also conceptualized the body as a "natural" phenomenon that lies outside their analytical concerns.

Violence is an embodied practice and Messerschmidt's (2000, 2004) life-history research shows that body size helps determine the type of violence boys will use under certain conditions to "do masculinity." For example, Hugh, one of Messerschmidt's (2000) respondents, was a tall and muscular boy who fought older peers on the school playground who confronted him with masculinity challenges, such as trying to force him and his friends off a field because they wanted to play kick ball. Hugh also disliked teachers because he perceived them as a "form of authority" and he used his physical strength to challenge their power by throwing desks. Messerschmidt (2005, p. 205) discovered that "within the social setting of the school, Hugh's body became his primary resource for masculine power and esteem and simultaneously constructed his victims as subordinate."

Zack, another boy interviewed by Messerschmidt, did not have the physical stature to be masculine like the "cool guys" at his school. He was overweight and was continually rejected by girls he asked to date him. Consequently, due to his inability to "measure up" physically to his school's view of the "ideal masculine body," during his sixth-grade year, he started to sexually assault his six-year-old female cousin and did so for three years using nonviolent, manipulative techniques. According to Messerschmidt (2000, pp. 47–48),

> the control, power, and sexual arousal associated with the sexual domination of his youngest cousin provided Zack a contextually based masculine resource when other masculine resources were unavailable – he was now a "cool guy." The sexual violence provided a sense of masculine accomplishment and therefore heightened his masculine self-esteem.

Recent studies reveal that poor inner-city males also face "overwhelming challenges" to their sense of masculinity, which, in turn, results in many of them engaging in street violence under certain situations (Anderson, 2008; Mullins, 2006). Of course, too, as stated in Chapter 2, critical criminologists, such as Perry (2003), show that racist and homophobic violence are also techniques of "doing masculinity." What makes her contribution even more important is that it constitutes a rigorous effort to address "the paucity of hate crime scholarship" within critical criminology (Perry, 2006, p. 155). So does DeKeseredy, Perry, and Schwartz's (2007) representative sample survey of hate-motivated sexual assaults on female undergraduates at two Ontario institutions of higher learning, which is the first Canadian study of its kind. They found that about 11 percent of the 384 women in their sample stated that they experienced one or more of five variants of hate-motivated sexual assault (e.g., sexual relations because of threats or actual use of force) in the past seven months. Ironically, while Canadian universities and colleges contribute to the advancement of learning and broadening of young minds, DeKeseredy *et al.*'s findings support Ehrlich's (1999) claim that these postsecondary institutions are showing dramatic trends towards intolerance, as evidenced by ongoing and even escalating rates of racial, ethnic, and gender harassment. Some US studies have uncovered similar problems on college campuses (e.g., Southern Poverty Law Center, 2003; Van Dyke and Tester, 2008).

Thinking critically about crimes like interpersonal violence entails taking a broader view. Comparative research is a prime example of such an approach and frequently involves examining data on two or more societies. Well known for his work on violence in US society,[4] left realist Elliott Currie (2008a) examined world-wide data on serious acts of interpersonal violence, such as murder. What makes his comparative research novel is that he points to the variability of violence around the world in recent years. For example, based on an analysis of World Health Organization data (see Krug *et al.*, 2002), Colombia and El Salvador "top the list" in murder, with rates of over 60 per 100,000 population in the former and more than 55 per 100,000 in the latter. At the other extreme are countries like Sweden, Ireland, and Greece, with homicide rates at or below the level of 1 per 100,000. Currie's research also shows that except for the United States, richer countries have lower rates of homicide than poorer nations.

Physical and sexual violence, of course, is not only found on the streets, in pubs and taverns, or in domestic/household settings. It is frequently directed at different types of animals (e.g., pets, strays, and livestock) (DeGue and DiLillo, 2008; Merz-Perez and Heide, 2004), at females during the filming of pornographic films or videos (Jensen, 2007), in workplaces (DeKeseredy, 2009b), and elsewhere. Critical criminologists are starting to examine these other harms that are often unnoticed, unreported, or ignored. In addition, although not generally viewed as violent, feminist criminologists have generated much data on offenses that cause just as much, if not more, harm than nonlethal acts of physical violence. Major examples of such behaviors are sexual harassment in private and public domains and coercive control in intimate relationships. Coercive control frequently involves psychologically and emotionally abusive behaviors that are often subtle, hard to detect and prove, and seem to be more forgivable to people unfamiliar with the abuse of women and its consequences. Two prime examples are threatening looks and criticism (Kernsmith, 2008). Many men also use other tactics of coercive control to suppress their intimate female partner's personal freedom, including "microregulating a partner's behavior" (Stark, 2007, p. 229). This, then, is another key reason why many feminist and other critical scholars assert that we should develop and operationalize even broader definitions of interpersonal violence.

CRIMES OF THE POWERFUL[5]

In his book, *Dude, Where's My Country*, film-maker Michael Moore (2003) states, "The fear drug works like this: You are repeatedly told that bad, scary people are going to kill you, so place all your trust in *us*, your corporate leaders, and we will protect you" (p. 138; emphasis in original). The reality is, however, that many corporate and political elites are "trusted criminals," and critical criminologists repeatedly remind us of this problem (Friedrichs, 2007). What Michalowski (1985) pointed out over 20 years ago still holds true today: "corporate crime represents the most widespread and costly form of crime in America" (p. 325). The same can be said about corporate crime in other parts of the world, such as Canada and the United Kingdom. For example, based on their review of the extant literature on corporate violence, some sociologists estimate that the rate of deaths from unsafe work conditions is more than six times greater than the street crime death rate, and the rate of nonlethal assault in the workplace is more than 30 times greater than the rate of predatory street assault (DeKeseredy, Ellis, and Alvi, 2005). Corporate violence is defined here as:

> any behavior undertaken in the name of the corporation by decision makers, or other persons in authority within the corporation, that endangers the health and safety of employees or other persons who are affected by that behavior. Even acts of omission, in which decision makers, etc., refuse to take action to reduce or eliminate known health and safety risks, must be considered corporate violence. It is the impact the action has on the victim, not the intent of the act, which determines whether or not it is violence.
>
> (DeKeseredy and Hinch, 1991, p. 100)

On top of documenting a host of corporate crimes, critical criminologists do extensive research on government or state crimes. One progressive scholar mentioned to David Kauzlarich and Rick Matthews (2006, p. 239) that "such a sustained body of high-quality scholarship from a network of researchers working in concert on a particular problem area was unparalleled in criminology." Nevertheless, defining state crime is subject to heated debates, which are not likely to be resolved soon. Still, most leading experts in the field agree with Rothe and Friedrichs' (2006) call for using international law as a "foundational basis" for understanding state crime, which includes standards such as human rights and social harms (Rothe, 2009).

Major examples of state crimes studied by contemporary critical criminologists include:

- genocidal rape in Rwanda (Mullins, 2009; Mullins and Rothe, 2008)
- child labor and violations of children's rights (Olsson, 2003)
- links between drug traffickers and political elites (Schulte-Bockholt, 2006)
- the Nazi Holocaust (Friedrichs, 2000; Matthews, 2006)
- violations of treaties between the US government and American-Indian tribes (Robyn, 2006)
- US army personnel torturing Iraqi prisoners at Abu Ghraib (N. Klein, 2007; Rothe, Kramer, and Mullins, 2009).

A much longer list of state crimes could be noted here. The same could be said about corporate crimes, which are types of white-collar crime (Friedrichs, 2007). White-collar and corporate crimes are similar in the sense that they occur in the context of occupational roles and are committed by "persons of high or respectable social status" (Helmkamp, Ball, and Townsend, 1996, p. 351). The major difference between the two crimes, however, is in the victims and beneficiaries of the crime. For example, corporate crime benefits both the company and the offender(s), while white-collar crime benefits only the offender. Corporate crime is thus defined here as "the conduct of employees acting on behalf of a corporation, which is proscribed and punishable by law" (Braithwaite, 1984, p. 6).

It is not always easy to distinguish between the two types of crime committed by executives because many corporate crimes also benefit the individuals. For example, executives who save their company money by insisting on maintaining unsafe working conditions for factory workers may be in line for a promotion to a higher salary. In general, though, white-collar crime is committed without the knowledge or permission of the company and is designed to profit only the individual (DeKeseredy et al., 2005). Corporate crime is, on the other hand, designed to benefit the company and only secondarily will profit the individual, if at all (DeKeseredy and Schwartz, 1996).

The most common technique of gathering data on crimes of the powerful, such as state and corporate crime, is the case study method (Matthews and Kauzlarich, 2006; Rothe et al., 2009; Tombs and Whyte, 2007). Case studies are detailed examinations of specific outcomes, events, or processes that occur over varying periods of time. Usually a single case is studied, such as the space shuttle Challenger explosion or the crash of ValuJet Flight 592 (Kramer, 2006; Matthews and Kauzlarich, 2006). Moreover, a variety of data collection methods may be used in conducting case studies, such as listening to and engaging in casual conversations, focused in-depth interviews, reviewing statistics, making tape recordings, taking photographs, making maps, and reading local newspapers, community notices, and records (Alvi, DeKeseredy, and Ellis, 2000).

A major obstacle facing all researchers is eliciting accurate data on the extent and distribution of crimes of the powerful. Some methods are better than others, but none of them can collect accurate data on the experiences of the thousands of North Americans who "continue to work, unaware that they are harboring slowly evolving occupational diseases or that physical ailments will painfully show themselves only after a great deal of accumulated damage is done" (Katz, 1978, p. 6). For this and other reasons, a few critical scholars claim that the victimization survey is an inappropriate means of uncovering reliable data from people harmed by crimes of the powerful that are often hidden or difficult to detect, such as the secretive dumping of toxic waste (Walklate, 1989).

Arguments such as this one are stated so often that they are considered by many to be truisms. Yet no concrete empirical evidence is presented that proves that the victimization survey is an inadequate mode of studying crimes such as corporate violence (DeKeseredy and Goff, 1992). Obviously, people cannot report incidents of unwitting victimization, such as exposure to particular pollutants (MacLean, 1991). This is a problem which no method can avoid, but as Friedrichs (2007, p. 37) puts it, "Surveys can contribute greatly to our under-standing of white collar crime because we still have much to learn about patterns of involvement, rationalizations, and atti-tudes pertaining to white collar crime issues." Left realists cer-tainly agree and those among them who conducted the second sweep of the Islington Crime Survey (ICS II) in the London Borough of Islington uncovered reliable and valid information on three variants of what Pearce (1992) refers to as commercial crime: workplace hazards, unlawful trading practices, and the victimization of housing tenants (Crawford, Jones, Woodhouse, and Young, 1990).

It is beyond the scope of this chapter to provide a detailed description of the data generated by the 1988 ICS II; however, based upon some of the findings reported by Pearce (1992), they provide a much more realistic account of the number of accidents people experience in the workplace than official British statistics did at that time. For example, then, the acci-dent rate per 100,000 workers was found to be approximately

30 times the national average. Another relevant victimization survey was conducted in the United States by the National White Collar Crime Center. Data gathered from a national survey of 1,169 US households showed that more than one out of every three households was victimized in 1999 by fraud through the following offenses:

• Internet transactions
• unauthorized use of their credit cards
• use of 800 or 900 telephone numbers
• unauthorized use of a personal identification number
• a free prize or vacation that turned out not to be free
• a free product sample that turned out not to be free (Rebovich and Layne, 2000).

Arguably, studying crimes of the powerful presents more challenges than collecting data on many "conventional crimes," such as juvenile delinquency. For example, it would be extremely difficult, if not impossible, to get a dictator who ordered the mass execution of citizens who opposed him or her to participate in an in-depth interview for social scientific purposes. Further, there is no crimes-of-the-powerful database equivalent to those maintained for street crimes (e.g., Uniform Crime Reports), and government agencies are uncomfortable funding research that may "hit too close to home" (Friedrichs, 2007). Yet, critical criminologists around the world persist in studying topics such as those briefly covered here and are heavily engaged in developing new ways of gathering data on genocide, price fixing, false advertising, child labor, and a myriad of other crimes of the powerful. For example, Rothe *et al.* (2009a) suggest the creation of a state crime database that takes the following approach:

• delineate the variables available: the scope of the enterprise (e.g., country, years, etc.);
• make a short list of hypotheses and variables that are important to gather data on;
• cull through existing databases (e.g., Human Rights Watch, Amnesty International, Transaction, Polity II, etc.);

- develop a search strategy for missing cases and variables;
- perform relevant statistical tests on hypotheses.

Lynch and Stretesky (2001) provide another example of a novel way of studying crimes of the powerful. They show us the value of examining medical evidence to identify toxic harms, such as hazardous waste. Undoubtedly, such important data cannot be gleaned from police statistics and other criminal justice databases.

In sum, critical criminological research shows that many people assumed to have what Jackson Toby (1957) refers to as a strong "stake in conformity" engage in behaviors that actually do more harm, cost more money, and destroy more lives than predatory street crimes such as mugging, theft, and so on (Reiman and Leighton, 2010). Some types of social control (e.g., policing), too, frequently cause much harm, and it is to recent critical research on this issue that I turn to next.

SOCIAL CONTROL

Critical criminology is well known for pointing to how certain laws and various techniques of social control are tools used by powerful social groups to promote and protect their interests. Particularly during the 1970s and 1980s, scholars such as Richard Quinney (1975), Frank Pearce (1976), William Chambliss (1986), and Colin Goff and Charles Reasons (1978) played an important role in sensitizing us to the class-based nature of the origins and functions of law. Marxist analyses of law and social control are still used today (e.g., Reiman and Leighton, 2010); however, some new theoretical perspectives emerged near the start of this century (e.g., critical race theory), as well as some new empirical directions (Friedrichs, 2001, 2009). On top of constantly showing the failures of the prison system and that those at the bottom of the socioeconomic ladder are more likely to be charged, convicted, and sent to prison, progressive scholars now devote much more attention to how gender and race/ethnicity shape law and social control. Some recent examples are Susan Miller's (1999) multi-method, feminist study of the impact of gender on community policing in a Midwestern

US city. For some readers, such a study may not appear unique, but most policing research still ignores gender and how it is related to police organizations and culture (Corsianos, 2009).

There is also a paucity of research on policing Native American communities, which is of paramount concern to Canadian critical criminologist Barbara Perry (2009b). Her interviews with 278 Native Americans from seven states in the United States reveal that police "under- and over-enforce" the law in Native American communities. In other words, Perry's respondents reported that the police would often turn a blind eye to their victimization, as well as subject them to violence and harassment. There is a large body of knowledge on racist police practices, but most of the extant US literature addresses the plight of African-Americans and Latinos. Thus, like Miller (1999), Perry has opened up a new door on critical inquiry.

The same can be said about the small group of critical criminologists who study crime and social control in rural communities. For example, DeKeseredy and Schwartz's (2009) Ohio study shows that rural male-to-female violence is seldom reported to the police, and when it is, these law-enforcement officials often respond in ways described by one of their respondents:

> Well, out here we deal with the Sheriff's Department outside the city limits. It would be nice if the deputies would stop rolling their eyeballs. You know, it's, uh, I don't think they treat domestic fights with enough seriousness.... I would like for the lawyers and the Sherriff's Department to be a little more sympathetic.
>
> (p. 9)

This response on the part of the legal system is not limited to rural areas. It is well known that many urban police officers ignore the plight of battered women and sexual assault survivors (Iovanni and Miller, 2001). Still, research such as that done by DeKeseredy and Schwartz (2009) and Websdale (1998) reveals that while there is a system of social practices that generally dominates and oppresses rural and urban women alike, it operates differently in rural areas. For example, people in urban communities often complain of feeling anonymous, victims of an uncaring mysterious policing system. In rural communities, violent men are more likely to be protected by an "ol' boys network" (Websdale, 1998). Many women know that the local police not only may be friends of their abusers, but also may refuse to arrest them on the grounds of this friendship (DeKeseredy and Joseph, 2006; Zorza, 2002). Critical scholarship in Australia also shows that the police are not likely to arrest men who abuse female intimates (Hogg and Carrington, 2006).

Within criminology, there is a rich history of observing police work (e.g., Manning, 1997; Skolnick, 1966). Still, until recently, mainstream and critical criminologists alike did not directly observe private policing or "parapolicing." George Rigakos (2002) notes in his book on this topic, "After an extensive literature review I could not locate a single published study of private police that examined the *doing* of security work from the perspective of line officers" (p. 3; emphasis in original). Informed by four bodies of knowledge (risk society, governmentality, Marxist analyses, and pluralist),[6] Rigakos conducted a first-hand ethnographic study of the Intelligarde International parapolice in Toronto,[7] one that addresses the importance of carefully examining the rapidly expanding nature of private policing and how variations of it (e.g., nightclub bouncers) are influenced by broader social forces, such as the capitalist political economy.

If policing is a major focus of critical criminologists, so are courts. New directions in critical research on this topic include Rothe and Mullins' (2006) work on the International Criminal Court (ICC), which also offers an integrated theoretical model of state crime originally developed by Kramer and Michalowski (see Kramer, Michalowski, and Kauzlarich, 2002). Feminists, too, are breaking new ground in court research. For example, Dragiewicz and DeKeseredy (2008) recently conducted a needs assessment and gap analysis for abused women unrepresented in the family law system that helped establish an empirical foundation for policy and programs that serve abused mothers in Ontario, Canada. Despite the frequency of anecdotal reports about problems with family law issues following separation and divorce and a growing awareness of problems for abused women in the family courts around custody, access, and child support, there is still little empirical research in Canada on the experiences of abused women who try to navigate the family law system without legal representation. As an exploratory study, Dragiewicz and DeKeseredy's study answered some important questions and raised many others that need to be addressed in much-needed further research on the topic.

Today, we are also witnessing a growth in feminist research on alternatives to the traditional court system, such as restorative justice in response to violence against women (Ptacek, 2010c). "Race matters" (West, 2001) and new feminist scholarship on restorative justice pays more than just lip service to this concern. For example, included in Ptacek's (2010c) anthology on restorative justice and violence against women are chapters that highlight the importance of carefully examining the implications of restorative justice in Aboriginal communities and in communities of color (e.g., Goel, 2010; Smith, 2010). Nonetheless, regardless of the area of criminal justice inquiry, much more research on the experiences of Asians and other ethnic minority groups is needed. Certainly, most of the critical scholarship produced so far on the relationship between race/ethnicity and legal systems focuses on the plight of blacks (Gabbidon and Greene, 2005), especially work done in the United States.

Critical criminologists, among others (e.g., some journalists), make it clear that there is no "freedom and justice for all" and that the primary targets of criminal justice attention are those at the bottom of the socioeconomic ladder (Lynch *et al.*, 2000; Reiman and Leighton, 2010). This is not to say, however, that the crimes socially and economically disenfranchised people commit are totally harmless. For example, many women are targets of brutal sexual and physical assaults committed by their current or former impoverished male partners (DeKeseredy, Alvi, Schwartz, and Tomaszewski, 2003; Renzetti and Maier, 2002). These and other crime victims (e.g., those harmed by "gay bashing") warrant much empirical, theoretical, and political attention. So does another group of victims that is "rarely in the limelight" (Radelet, 2005). These are, as Susan Sharp (2005) uncovered, the "hidden victims" of the death penalty in the United States. Her in-depth interviews with families of those facing a death sentence are not only innovative, but also reveal much pain and suffering that goes unnoticed.

As one interviewee described to Sharp, her mother was "terribly damaged" after her son's execution:

> It is ... difficult for me to see my mother suffer like she does. She goes to the cemetery often and sits for hours. Sometimes she won't take off her pajamas nor answer her phone. My brother's room is still like it was when he left.... She lives in guilt every day and she is beating herself up for it. She feels totally responsible and she is punishing herself. Her health is failing fast, and she is going to have a heart attack one of these days.
>
> (p. 103)

The death penalty, or the possibility of receiving it, is not the only criminal justice sanction that harms families. For example, in most impoverished urban neighborhoods in the United States, as many as 20 percent of adult males are incarcerated on any given day, and almost every family has a father, son, brother, or uncle who has been in a correctional facility (Clear, 2007). Critical research shows that families impacted by such mass incarceration experience many major problems. In the words of Travis and Waul (2003, pp. 1–2):

> To begin with, families impacted by incarceration are already typically at high risk along several dimensions. A parent's incarceration does not necessarily signal the onset of family and child development needs, but rather in most cases adds to the burdens of a family already struggling to overcome life's obstacles and setbacks. The incarceration of a family member may further exacerbate an environment already characterized by ongoing poverty, stress, and trauma.

Many neighborhoods, too, are also hidden victims of mass incarceration, especially inner-city slums populated primarily by African-Americans. The concentration of ex-convicts in poor communities not only precludes many of them from finding legitimate work because they are "marked" (Pager, 2007), but also harms the labor market prospects of others in the neighborhood, as well as affecting the voting patterns and election outcomes in some communities. Approximately one million Florida citizens are banned from voting for life because of a previous felony conviction, and 50 percent of them are African-American (Clear, 2007). Mass incarceration also increases the number of female-headed, single-parent families on welfare, which contributes to much stigmatization and isolation from conventional society (Browne, 1997; Clear, 2007; Wilson, 1996). Such research highlights the importance of bringing economic disadvantage and social exclusion back into public discussions and policies about crime (Vogel, 2007).

THE MEDIA[8]

Since its inception, critical criminology has attended to how the media contributes to crime, perceptions and meanings of crime, and to social control. Undeniably, in the words of cultural criminologists Ferrell *et al.* (2008), the study of crime and the media is a "well-trodden path" (p. 125). This is not to say, though, that media never change and that critical criminologists and other researchers do not adapt and respond to ongoing transformations, such as the creation of YouTube, Facebook, etc. As communications scholar Joseph Walther and his colleagues observed nearly 10 years ago,

> With the expansion of the Internet and new communications technologies, we are witnessing the diffusion of high-end, high bandwidth multimedia technology for a wide range of people. It is common for many computer-mediated communication (CMC) users to create multi-media World Wide Web sites with graphics and pictures.
>
> (p. 105)

This statement is still relevant and many such sites are beneficial to corporate executives, small business owners, educators, students, and to a myriad of other people eager to enhance their understanding of social, political, cultural, and economic factors that directly or indirectly influence their lives. However, critical scholars identify some highly injurious features of new information technologies, one of which is adult Internet pornography.

Today, we live in a "post-*Playboy* world" (Jensen, 2007), where defining adult pornography is still subject to much debate. Those who produce adult pornography, consume it, and/or oppose prohibiting it typically define harmful, sexually explicit material as erotica. However, there is a big difference between erotica and adult pornography. Erotica refers to "sexually suggestive or arousing material that is free of sexism, racism, and homophobia and is respectful of all human beings and animals portrayed" (Russell, 1993, p. 3). On the other hand, in adult pornography:

> Women are represented as passive and as slavishly dependent upon men. The role of female characters is limited to the provision of sexual services to men. To the extent that women's sexual pleasure is represented at all, it is subordinated to that of men and is never an end itself as is the sexual pleasure of men. What pleases men is the use of their bodies to satisfy male desires. While the sexual objectification of women is common to all pornography, in which women characters are killed, tortured, gang-raped, mutilated, bound, and otherwise abused, as a means of providing sexual stimulation or pleasure to the male characters.
>
> (Longino, 1980, p. 42)

Many women consume adult pornography, but it is created primarily for generating sexual arousal in heterosexual men (Jensen, 2007). From the standpoint of many feminist scholars (e.g., DeKeseredy, 2009b; Dworkin, 1994), pornography, regardless of whether it appears on the Internet, in stores, on television, in literature, or in other media, is also a variant of hate-motivated violence and it, too, has become "normalized" or "mainstreamed" in North America and elsewhere (Jensen and Dines, 1998), despite becoming increasingly more violent and racist (DeKeseredy, 2009b).

It is beyond the scope of this chapter to graphically describe what appears on contemporary pornographic Internet sites, but some brief examples of violence and racism are necessary. For instance, Doghouse Digital is a company that produced the film *Black Bros and White Ho's*, which offers stereotypical images of "the sexually primitive black male stud" (Jensen, 2007, p. 66).

Another example is the interracial film *Blacks on Blondes*, which features a white man in a cage watching black men have sex with his wife (Dines, 2006). An additional common feature of new pornographic films that exist online and elsewhere is painful anal penetration, as well as men slapping women and/or pulling their hair while they penetrate them orally, vaginally, and/or anally (Dines and Jensen, 2008a). Also, many pornographic Internet sites routinely depict black, Asian, Hispanic, and women from other social groups (e.g., those with disabilities) in hurtful ways.

Perhaps "normalized" is an understatement. Pornography is a giant industry and it is estimated that there are over one million pornography sites on the Internet, with as many as 10,000 added every week (Funk, 2006). Note, too, that worldwide pornography revenues from a variety of sources (e.g., Internet, hotel rooms, etc.) recently topped $97 billion. This is more than the revenues of these world-renowned technology companies combined: Microsoft, Google, Amazon, eBay, Yahoo!, Apple, Netflix, and Earthlink (Zerbisias, 2008). Another key point to consider is that rare are men who are not exposed to pornographic images and narratives on the Internet (DeKeseredy and Olsson, in press; Schwartz and DeKeseredy, 1997). Even if people go out of their way to avoid pornography, it frequently "pops up" on people's monitors while they are working or "surfing the web" for information that has nothing to do with sex (Dines and Jensen, 2008b).

To make matters worse, as noted above, contemporary critical criminological research shows that what men and boys watch on adult pornographic Internet sites are not simply "dirty pictures that have little impact on anyone." Rather, the images typically endorse "women as second-class citizens" and "require that women be seen as second-class citizens" (Funk, 2006, p. 165). Another challenge to the assertion that "pornography is just fantasy" are quantitative and qualitative data showing that pornography is strongly associated with various types of violence against women (DeKeseredy, in press a; Jensen, 2007), especially sexual assault. In addition, some studies found that the contribution of pornography to woman abuse in dating, marriage, and during or after separation/

divorce is related to male peer support (DeKeseredy and Schwartz, 2009). For example, many violent, patriarchal men often view pornography in all-male groups and share videos and other media electronically with a "wider circle of friends" via the Internet (DeKeseredy, in press a; Giordano, 1995).

Contemporary critical criminologists uncover misogyny and racism in other media, such as modern rap music (Weitzer and Kubrin, 2009). For Patricia Hill Collins (2000), rap is seen as one of the modern "controlling images" used to oppress black women, and Oliver (2006) asserts that rap's patriarchal or sexist lyrics "provide justifications for engaging in acts of violence against black women" (p. 927). However, Weitzer and Kubrin (2009) contend that such music is a method of controlling all women because it is consumed by a diverse range of youth. For cultural criminologists Ferrell *et al.* (2008), contemporary rap music also "embodies the evolving fusion of crime and consumerism, of transgression and popular art" (p. 139).

Race/ethnicity is an important factor for critical criminologists who study Western media representations of terrorism, which, not surprisingly, gained much attention after September 11, 2001. In-depth analyses of numerous fictional and non-fictional media accounts of events such as 9/11 reveal a "troubling absence of Muslim perspectives," while simultaneously perpetuating and legitimating racist stereotypes of Muslims (Chermak, Bailey, and Brown, 2003, p. 5; Strawson, 2003).

As well as studying how crime is "spun," another group of critical criminologists challenge racist, sexist, and other media-produced stereotypes of crime and criminals by disseminating their own interpretations and arguments through the media, an approach referred to as "newsmaking criminology" (Barak, 1988, 1995b). Since newspapers, television shows, web sites, and magazines reach large audiences, newsmaking criminologists assert that progressive scholars and activists should take every opportunity to offer their research and views to the media, creating a situation where they are "seen and heard, not after the fact, but proactively" (Renzetti, 1999, p. 1236). That articles and letters written by critical criminologists are periodically published by the mainstream press and that some critical scholars have been on television serves as evidence that the media do not totally dismiss or ignore struggles against patriarchal, capitalist, and racist oppression (Caringella-MacDonald and Humphries, 1998; DeKeseredy *et al.*, 2003).

Newsmaking criminology is often vaguely distasteful to academics socialized in an atmosphere of supposedly value-free positivism, even when they intellectually reject their training (Brownstein, 1991). Academics are frequently taught that their job is just to announce the facts, then stand back and allow the politicians and activists to debate and use these "facts" (Schwartz and DeKeseredy, 1997). Unfortunately, the world of understanding is largely a symbolic one where reality is constructed and negotiated (Goodwin, 1983). The struggle to define the "typical case," often called by sociologists *typification*, is an essential one. The group that is most successful in setting up the facts that are recognized in the minds of politicians and the general public as being examples of the problem is going to be the group most likely to have an effect upon the development of the solution (Best, 1990; Schwartz and DeKeseredy, 1993).

SUMMARY

Critical criminologists produce qualitative and quantitative scholarship accounting for both sides of the power equation: how crimes of the powerful are exempt from the purview of the law; and how the powerless become criminalized (DeKeseredy and Perry, 2006b). Similarly, critical criminologists offer rich data on various types of interpersonal violence and media representations of crime, law, and social control. As stated at the beginning of this chapter, these scholars also study topics outside the realm of criminology (e.g., Amish social life). The main objective of this chapter was to offer some recent examples of empirical criminological work done by progressive colleagues. Hopefully, this brief overview of contemporary research will help challenge the myth of critical criminology as simply a critique of mainstream contributions.

Contrary to what many people claim, critical criminologists do not outright reject quantitative methods. In fact, some left-wing scholars frequently use them. Further, many critical criminologists devote considerable time and effort to reading scholarship generated by mainstream scholars for several reasons, one of which is to determine if their empirical contributions have the potential to inform a more progressive understanding of social problems. Rarely, however, is critical research, regardless of whether it is quantitative or qualitative, cited in widely read and cited mainstream journals. Keep in mind the following observation made by David Kauzlarich (2006) in his Foreword to Rothe and Mullins' (2006, p. x) book, *Symbolic Gestures and the Generation of Global Social Control*:

> Hagan and Greer's (2002) article in *Criminology*, among the most prestigious journals in the field, examines the ebb and flow of international criminal justice as it pertains to war crimes and crime against humanity. The authors provide only one brief citation of critical criminological work on these subjects, ignoring the important work that Rothe and Mullins have thoroughly documented and expanded upon in Chapter 1 of this book. How the Hagan and Greer article was published in such a major journal without any attention to, to name a few, the work of Bill Chambliss (1989), Gregg Barak (1991), Ken Tunnell (1993), and Jeffrey Ian Ross (1995, 2000a, 2000b) can only be explained by author, editor, and reviewer unfamiliarity and/or indifference to the work of critical criminologists.

Some readers might add to Kauzlarich's commentary that critical criminology is sharply ridiculed by most mainstream researchers. Regardless of why progressive scholarship receives limited attention in traditional circles, it definitely has much to offer and reflects thoughtful attempts to advance a rigorous empirical understanding of social problems. Moreover, "mutual respect and supportiveness" are key characteristics of the critical criminological community (Friedrichs, 1996), which is a major reason there will be an explosion of new progressive scholarship on a broad range of topics in the coming decades.

4

CONFRONTING CRIME[1]

CRITICAL CRIMINOLOGICAL POLICIES

I am forced to conclude that the fundamental inhumanity of penal confinement and the corresponding processes of "otherizing" diminishes all human beings – whether they are female or male.

(Owen, 2005, p. 285)

As stated previously, the United States has shifted from a "welfare state" to a "penal state" (Wacquant, 2001). So have other countries, including Canada, a nation deemed by many people around the world as much more progressive than the United States. For example, staunch "law and order" advocate and Progressive Conservative Member of Parliament Stephen Harper was elected Prime Minister in 2006. Not coincidently, Canada's incarceration rate increased for the first time in more than a decade in 2005/2006. An average of 33,123 adults and 1,987 youths were then in custody, which was 3 percent more than in 2004/2005 (Statistics Canada, 2007b). Imprisonment is also racialized in Canada. While men of color constitute only 0.02 percent of Canada's population and 0.03 percent of the province of Ontario's population, they account for more than 5 percent of the federal institution population and 11 percent of Ontario's institution population (DeKeseredy, 2009a; Griffiths, 2007). Aboriginal people are also overrepresented in Canadian penal institutions. Aboriginals account for only 2 percent of the adult Canadian population, but they represent 14 percent of federal inmates and 18 percent of their provincial/territorial counterparts (Terrill, 2007).

Chesney-Lind's (2007) commentary on the shift from welfare state to penal state in the United States is therefore also relevant to Canada: "Along with this shift, of course, comes public attitudes about crime issues and criminals that reinforce prison as a viable 'solution' to the many social problems associated with this nation's long struggle with racial justice and income inequality" (p. 212). Note that although the Canadian homicide rate dropped by 10 percent in 2006 compared to 2005 (Li, 2007), one of the Harper government's slogans at that time was "Serious Crime = Serious Time" and it passed the omnibus Tackling Violent Crime Act on February 28, 2008, parts of which "mimic failed US methods" (Travers, 2007), such as the "three-strikes, you're out" sentencing law.[2]

Twenty-six US states and the US federal government now have three-strikes laws. The Canadian federal government's push for similar legislation occurred at roughly the same time Toronto was designated as "Canada's poverty capital" (Monsebraaten and Daly, 2007). There, at that time, close to 30 percent of families (about 93,000 households raising children) lived in poverty, which was a 16 percent increase since 1990 (United Way of Greater Toronto, 2007). It is likely that a sizeable portion of Toronto's poor will soon end up in jail or prison in response to their use of drugs to cope with the daily life-events stress spawned by being socially and economically excluded.

Did the Tackling Violent Crime Act make a difference after it was passed in 2008? Yes, but not in the ways anticipated by proponents of getting "tough on crime." In 2008, there were 611 homicides in Canada, 17 more than in 2007. This constituted a 2 percent increase in the national murder rate. Furthermore, there were 200 homicides committed with a firearm during the same year, 12 more than in 2007. The rate of homicides committed with a firearm also increased by 24 percent since 2002 (Statistics Canada, 2009). These and similar findings support Currie's (2008a) claim that taking a more punitive approach to crime frequently results in higher levels of violence.

Would more progressive or more liberal leaders call for less punitive measures and help cure the "addiction to incarceration" that plagues the United States and other countries, such as the Russian Federation (Pratt, 2009)?[3] This question is partially answered in Chapter 1, but a more detailed response is warranted. Undeniably, there is no evidence of a rapidly growing penal abolition movement in the United States. For example, so-called liberal Bill Clinton did not let the Republicans "out-tough him on crime" when he ran for president in the United States in 1992 (Chesney-Lind, 2007, p. 212). He interrupted his New Hampshire campaign to preside over the execution of mentally disabled Rickey Ray Rector in Arkansas (Sherrill, 2001). North of the US border, in fall 2007, Stephan Dion, then Canadian Liberal Leader of the Official Opposition, also did not want to be "out-toughed on crime" (DeKeseredy, 2009b). The minority government led by Stephen Harper could have easily fallen had Dion called for a parliamentary nonconfidence vote on the Tackling Violent Crime Act. However, he lacked confidence about going into a fall 2007 election and did not want to "trigger one by defeating the populist law-and-order agenda of the Conservatives" (Hebert, 2007, p. A17).

Although very popular among liberal circles, US President Barak Obama doesn't appear to have reducing the incarceration rate and/or eliminating the death penalty on his list of priorities for similar reasons. Perhaps, too, like many people raised in the United States, he grew up in a conservative political economic climate which precludes him from seeing any alternatives to the crime problem beyond the punitive status quo (Chesney-Lind, 2007). It also appears that universities and colleges are not doing much to encourage criminal justice students to think more critically about crime. For example, research done at several US institutions of higher learning reveals that criminal justice students were "more punitive in their attitudes toward crime, criminals, and the criminal justice system" (Courtright, MacKey, and Packard, 2005, p. 140).

So, what is to be done? An obvious, but simplistic, critical criminological answer to this question is radical social, political, and economic change, such as a transition from a capitalist, patriarchal society to one that is socialist and feminist. True, outrageous problems often require outrageous solutions (Gibbons, 1995), but few critical criminologists believe that truly fundamental changes will occur soon in the United States, Canada, and other countries with a similar political economic order. In fact, there is ample evidence that many parts of the world are "moving in precisely the wrong directions" if the goal is to curb violence and other serious crimes (Currie, 2008a, p. 112). As briefly mentioned in Chapter 2, unbridled, "laissez-faire" economic policies are aggressively implemented in North America and elsewhere. As Currie (2008a, pp. 112–113) observes:

> The social arrangements that are characteristic of the most dangerous societies are now, in many places, being enshrined as fundamental virtues: the tolerance of great inequality in the name of economic growth; a willingness to let individuals and families fall into extreme deprivation in the name of encouraging "personal responsibility"; a willingness to leave people's well-being up to the fluctuations of the job market; the shrinking of public supports for the vulnerable in the name of boosting self-reliance and ending dependency.

There is substantial empirical support for Currie's claim. Yet, bigger gaps between the rich and poor, a rabid anti-feminist backlash, government-supported assaults on affirmative action programs, and the like do not weaken critical criminologists' resolve. They continue to propose progressive short-term strategies that chip away at the forces that motivate people to commit crime and that buttress unequal justice. Of course, thousands of alternatives to the status quo could be listed but will not be. Moreover, many readers will notice that conspicuously absent from this chapter are in-depth accounts of how initiatives such as progressive criminal justice reforms, job creation and training, a higher minimum wage, state-sponsored child care, and housing assistance help curb crime. These important strategies are briefly discussed here, but they are not new suggestions and have been covered at length in previous critical criminological books. The main objective of this chapter is not to repeat in detail what has already been proposed, but rather to supplement these suggestions with more contemporary initiatives. The key, though, is to recognize that we must take on these tasks. As Irwin and Austin (1994, p. 167) pointed out nearly 20 years ago:

> Reducing crime means addressing those factors that are more directly related to crime. This means reducing teenage pregnancies, high school dropout rates, unemployment, drug abuse, and lack of meaningful job opportunities. Although many will differ on how to address these factors, the first step is to acknowledge that these forces have far more to do with reducing crime than escalating the use of imprisonment.

CRIMINAL JUSTICE REFORMS

Critical criminologists propose many progressive criminal justice reforms, ranging from democratic accountability of the police (Kinsey, Lea, and Young, 1986), to legalizing the production and sale of "illicit drugs" (Reiman and Leighton, 2010), to stricter legislation aimed at reducing corporate crime. A more recent concern for some scholars who study interpersonal violence is the criminal justice system's response to ice hockey violence (DeKeseredy, in press a), especially the types that occur during National Hockey League games in North America. One widely publicized event that still remains in the minds of many professional hockey fans is former Vancouver Canucks player Todd Bertuzzi's vicious attack on former Colorado Avalanche player Steve Moore on March 8, 2004. From behind, Bertuzzi grabbed Moore's jersey and punched him in the side of his head (an attack that is readily available on the video-sharing website YouTube). Following this assault, several members of both teams, including Bertuzzi, jumped on Moore. Moore suffered major injuries and will never play professional hockey again. Should those who commit acts like Bertuzzi's be labeled violent criminals? Or, are their potentially lethal behaviors "just part of the game"? Many people obviously agree with this statement because Bertuzzi received no criminal record from this incident and went on to play for Team Canada in the 2006 Winter Olympics.

Only a small number of cases such as the assault on Steve Moore have resulted in litigation. Thus, it is fair to conclude that despite the life-threatening nature of some "punch-ups," many people see nothing wrong with "hockey fisticuffs" (Smith, 1983). On the other hand, a growing number of critical criminologists are teaming up with nonprofit organizations (e.g., Canadian Paraplegic Association Ontario) and journalists to demand that the justice system help end hockey violence. As is the case with corporate crime, professional hockey players' crimes on the ice should be responded to as vigorously as predatory street crime. If not, in the words of Toronto sports journalist Dave Perkins (2010, p. S4), "it won't be long now until a hockey player dies on the ice from a stupid and vicious head hit, the kind that show no signs of ceasing any time soon as the game's higher levels."

Some critical criminologists also call for the criminalization of another form of violence that is exempt from prosecution in most countries – the spanking of children. Spanking is the most universal type of physical violence (DeKeseredy, 2009c), but it is illegal in Sweden, Finland, Denmark, Norway, and Austria (Alvarez and Bachman, 2008). There are sound reasons for strictly prohibiting it. For example, spanking is strongly associated with other forms of violence, such as bullying and violence against women in adult intimate relationships (Payne and Gainey, 2006). Further, spanking and other frequent types of physical punishment (e.g., slapping), teach children these four lessons:

- Love is associated with violence, and those who love you also have the right to hurt you.
- Physical punishment is used to train the child, which establishes the moral rightness of hitting other family members.
- When something is really important, it justifies the use of physical force.
- When one is under stress, tense, or angry, hitting is understandable and, to a certain extent, legitimate (Johnson, 1996, p. 5).

Violent and other hurtful acts are also committed by states or governments, and some key examples were given in Chapter 3 (e.g., military personnel torturing prisoners). Thus, Rothe and Mullins (2006) call for legal reforms such as enhancing the jurisdiction of the International Criminal Court (ICC) to address crimes committed by governments and transnational corporations, as well as individuals. Furthermore, two of the major crimes they assert should be covered are state terrorism and "unilateral war mongering" (p. 113). Certainly, much more attention should be devoted to such harms, and Rothe and Mullins, among others (e.g., Friedrichs, 2007), remind us that critical criminological policies should be aimed at both crimes "at the top" and "crimes at the bottom."

FULL AND QUALITY EMPLOYMENT

In North America and other parts of the world once known for being manufacturing strongholds (e.g., Ontario, Canada), work is rapidly disappearing because of factors such as outsourcing of jobs to developing countries and the implementation of new technologies in the workplace. This is also a constant right-wing "race to deunionize" (Massey, 2007), as well as other major economic shifts that simultaneously increase unemployment rates and reduce the number of quality full-time jobs. These are not simply economic issues, because getting and holding a steady job reduces the risk of people committing crime. In fact, a high level of stable employment is one of the main reasons there was a major decline in US crime rates in the 1990s (Currie, 2008a). On the other hand, without meaningful and stable work, people are more prone to committing crimes for reasons outlined by left realists (e.g., relative deprivation) or to survive. For example, thefts and frauds committed by North American women tend to focus on meeting their economic needs or those of their families (Barker, 2009).

The great shortage of both jobs and quality employment not only influences many disenfranchised people to commit street crimes, but can also keep them from escaping being crime victims. For instance, although most battered women do leave their abusers (DeKeseredy and Schwartz, 2009), many unemployed women cannot leave right away because they do not have the money to house and feed themselves and their children (Raphael, 2009).

Some critical criminologists suggest specific ways to deal with these problems. Michalowski (1983), for example, proposed several policies aimed at reducing street crime that place financial burdens on industry rather than on taxpayers. They include:

- tax surcharges on industries attempting to close plants or permanently reduce a community's work force;
- government laws requiring retraining and job placement for all workers displaced by new technology;
- a minimum wage level that is approximately 50 percent higher than the poverty level.

(pp. 14–18)

As we progress through this new millennium, these and somewhat similar initiatives continue to be suggested by an international body of critical criminologists. The problem, and the most discouraging aspect of making such recommendations, is not that political and corporate elites are uncaring or neglectful in their failure to invest in decent, full-time employment. Rather, especially in the United States, they aggressively oppose such policies, even when they are confronted with evidence that these and similar strategies work. Conservative politicians and corporations resist job creation and training initiatives because they do not want to lose the financial gains they have made under the current system (Barak, 1986). In other words, it isn't so much economic obstacles as ideological ones that account for the failure to mount a massive campaign to expand and upgrade the labor force.

HIGHER MINIMUM WAGE

Many countries, such as the United States, have social policies that coerce people into low-paying, "dead end jobs" to help lower embarrassing official unemployment rates (Currie, 2008a). Since many of the "working poor" are not making a decent wage, it is amazing how they survive in the face of being "nickel and dimed" (Ehrenreich, 2001). Hence, rather than continue down the worn path of reminding the working poor that "they are lucky to have a job," the minimum wage should be raised, which increases people's standard of living and reduces crime. For example, when a server in a fast-food restaurant works for a pay check that precludes him or her from eating properly so that the customer can eat more cheaply, this person will experience alienation, social exclusion, and relative deprivation (DeKeseredy, Alvi, Schwartz, and Tomaszewski, 2003), which are major correlates of crimes committed by disenfranchised people (Young, 1999). Moreover, low wages enable those involved in illegal work (e.g., drug dealing) to easily recruit new "employees" (Currie, 1993). For people "systematically deprived of access to avenues of success, how can the 'honest job' of dishwashing compete with the easy money obtained through dishonest behavior"? (Pfohl, 1994, p. 264).

SOCIAL SERVICES AND PROGRAMS

Conservative criminologists such as James Q. Wilson (1985) take much delight in pointing out that state-sponsored social services provided in the 1960s failed to reduce the crime rate in the United States and other capitalist nations. This is because most of the policies of the 1960s were not sensitive to the powerful influences of the political economy, community, and family. For example, in the United States, large numbers of youths were trained in the Job Corps for jobs that did not exist. However, few attempts were made to deal with the structural disintegration of troubled individuals' familial and neighborhood environments (Currie, 1985). It is not surprising that the failure of government-funded social programs was successfully exploited by conservative politicians to gain popular support for a policy of reducing social spending (DeKeseredy and Schwartz, 1996).

At the time of writing this book, conservative politicians are still cutting social programs and services, but claim that this agenda is designed to reduce government debt. As Canadian Prime Minister Stephen Harper stated on January 19, 2010, "As our recovery program comes to an end and we prepare to bring down the deficit once the economy has begun to grow again, it is essential that the government limit public spending" (cited in Whittington and Campion-Smith, 2010, p. A6). The trend in government today, as it was in the past two decades, supported by the media and by more and more voters, is to cut social services because we can't afford them, but at the same time dramatically increase spending on prisons. Much of the reason that many people support these notions is because they assume that the policies will not affect them; they will mainly affect visible minorities, such as African-Americans.

Stephen Harper and politicians with similar beliefs help fuel what Currie (2008a, p. 111) refers to as a *"culture of disregard,* in which people feel little sense of responsibility or solidarity toward others and a 'me-first' ethic of personal gain often dominates public life."* The reality is, though, that services such as early-childhood education, effective parenting training, prenatal care, affordable housing, and remedial education are worthwhile and help curb crime (Currie, 1985; DeKeseredy *et al.*, 2003). However, can those who participate in these programs be guaranteed financial security after they complete them (Currie, 1992)? History reveals that the answer to this question is an emphatic "no." For example, what is the point of going back to school or participating in job training if there is no chance of getting a job? To avoid repeating the mistakes of the 1960s, then, social programs and services must be accompanied by the elimination of unemployment and sub-employment.

USING NEW TECHNOLOGIES

Taylor, Walton, and Young's (1973) *The New Criminology* raised questions about the role that progressive scholars should play in the broader arena of political activism (Walton, 1998). Certainly, there are many political actions that do not cost much time, effort, and money. One example is using new computer technologies such as Facebook. For example, as of January 20, 2010, nearly 200,000 Canadians signed a Facebook petition protesting Prime Minister Harper's prorogation of Parliament on December 30, 2009. The Canadian legislature was originally set to reconvene on January 25, 2010, but Harper delayed the return until March 3, 2010. This prorogation eliminates bills tabled at the previous parliamentary session, including some related to important environmental and pension issues (Werbowski, 2010). Prorogation also shut down a public inquiry about the Harper government's knowledge of the torture of detainees handed over to Afghan forces by the Canadian military.

Social networking websites make a difference. Two weeks after the creation of the above petition, the Harper government's lead over the Liberal Party fell to only 1 percent (Hebert, 2010). This is strong evidence that new technologies are effectively used to mobilize large numbers of people to demand government accountability and to challenge attempts to cover up state crime and other state wrongdoings. Further, progressive Facebook initiatives are examples of reinvigorated civic engagement that are also being used to digitally protest white supremacy online (Daniels, 2009). Contrary to what many people claim, social networking sites are now key arenas of political struggle. As University of Bergen scholar Jill Walker Rettberg (2009, p. 1) observes:

> Obviously people find it easier to join a Facebook group to make a political point than to march the streets. Perhaps it's actually more effective, too. Right now, it's entirely possible that you get more press, and thus more national notice for a Facebook group with 2000 members than a demonstration of 500 people. And it's a *lot* easier to get 2000 people to join a Facebook group than to get 500 people to show up at a particular time and place with banners.

Using Facebook to help achieve social justice is a contemporary technique of newsmaking criminology that attracts more and more people each day. So are blogging and other new means of exchanging information. Communication is vital, and if Facebook, Twitter, etc. enable more people to become aware of various injustices, more people will voice their discontent with the prevailing inequitable status quo by electing politicians committed to a more progressive way of dealing with social problems such as crime. At the very least, such newsmaking criminology makes the issues covered in this book and in other sources very visible to the public in the same way that the above Canadian Facebook petition raised considerable public awareness about the problems related to the prorogation of Parliament.

BOYCOTTING HARMFUL COMPANIES[4]

Many companies are criminogenic and corporate crime is far more economically, physically, socially, and environmentally injurious than street crime (Reiman and Leighton, 2010). Further, corporations, such as satellite and cable companies, generate much profit from broadcasting hurtful pornographic images of men and women. Although formal agents of social control are quick to punitively respond to producers and consumers of "child porn," there is no reason to believe that government officials in a capitalist society are going to launch a "war on corporate crime" or adult pornographic television channels or videos in the near future. We seldom hear cries for "three strikes and you're out" in relation to corporate crime. In fact, some evidence suggests that governments around the world are making it easier for corporations to threaten our well-being.

Profit is a corporation's "bottom line." Thus, many people call for boycotting products and services offered by criminogenic companies or those that profit from legal means of causing harm, such as pornographic video stores. Boycotting has a long history and is not a contemporary critical criminological approach. Nevertheless, scholars and activists are using new means of boycotting. For example, since violent and racist pornography are "normalized," "mainstreamed," and easily accessible (Jensen and Dines, 1998), some feminist men's groups, such as the Minnesota Men's Action Network: Alliance to Prevent Sexual and Domestic Violence, participate in variations of the Clean Hotel Initiative.[5] This involves encouraging businesses, government agencies, private companies, and so on to only hold conferences and meetings in hotels that do not offer in-room adult pay-per-view pornography. Further, new groups of men and women join hands to collectively expose and criticize injurious media coverage of woman abuse (e.g., wife beating) and to boycott companies that profit from pornography. Robert Jensen (2007, p. 182) is right to state that "it's not enough for us to change our personal behavior. That's a bare minimum. Such change must be followed by participation in movements to change the unjust structure and the underlying ideology that supports them."

Such efforts make a difference because of their financial impact, but they are also accused of promoting censorship. Therefore, in efforts to formally and informally sensitize people to the harmful nature of pornography, such as boycotts, a few critical criminologists suggest that anti-pornography educators and activists should respond to claims of censorship by stating that there are many types of harmful films that cannot be found in hotels, video stores, and other places, mostly because they do not exist (DeKeseredy, in press a; DeKeseredy and Schwartz, 1998). Rather than constituting outright censorship, citizens of many countries manage to express their disgust and dismay at even the slight hint of harm to animals in motion pictures. Where the plot line requires an animal to be fictionally hurt (e.g., a great white shark eating a swimming dog),[6] Hollywood producers find it essential to report in the credits that their set was inspected and monitored by animal-rights organizations. Even then, however, there are virtually no movies that show animals burned, dismembered, stabbed or shot to death, electrocuted, beaten or kicked, or raped. These images are saved for stories about men and women.

Similarly, it is important to mention to those making claims about censorship that there are no movies available showing, in an approving manner, the mass execution of Jews, gypsies, and the mentally ill by the German Nazis in World War II. There are also no pro-slavery movies showing approvingly how white people need to beat, starve, and torture African slaves to get them to behave "properly." This is because people show a very high intolerance for movies of this nature being publicly available. Why is it that there are very firm reactions against seeing a dog raped, but it is found to be appropriate, or at least a free speech issue, to allow films approvingly showing women being beaten and gang raped by a group of men? Thus, there is a major point to be made to those who accuse opponents of pornography to be "pro-censorship": rather than calling for censorship, anti-porn activists argue that in a better society, it would be considered morally reprehensible to show or attend certain types of films, just as it is now for non-documentary films about animal torture, pro-slavery violence, or Nazi killings (DeKeseredy, in press a; DeKeseredy and Schwartz, 1998).

CREATING A CULTURE OF SUPPORT[7]

Currie (2004) identifies modern social Darwinist culture as a key determinant of many middle-class teenagers' troubles. What is to be done? He suggests progressive ways of developing a "culture of support," such as inclusive schools and offering troubled teenagers welcoming places to go when they leave or are thrown out of their homes. Currie's policy proposals make many people uncomfortable, given the extreme punitiveness of the United States. However, there is considerable support for these strategies. For example, Crespo's (1987) study of skipping school suggests that authorities would be more successful in preventing continued skipping and in reducing drop-out rates if stigmatizing, segregative measures were replaced by reintegrative ones. These could include positive recognition and acceptance of skippers when they do attend classes, pairing regular and conscientious attendees with skippers on school projects, support and reward of the participation of skippers in school activities they do enjoy (e.g., sports and music), and making the curriculum more relevant to the interests and capacities of skippers.

These approaches are examples of what Currie refers to as "inclusive discipline, in which the first priority is to understand why a student is having trouble and in which throwing kids out is the last resort, not the first" (p. 269). If school authorities base their reactions to student's troubles on an understanding of the causes, they may help de-amplify, or at least not amplify, students' use of drugs and involvement in other dangerous activities (DeKeseredy, Ellis, and Alvi, 2005). For example, Jarjoura (1993) found that skipping and dropping out are not in themselves predictors of troublemaking. Rather, the reasons for doing these things are more reliable predictors of delinquency. Hence, students who skip or drop out of school to help their parents or because of the problems at home are as conformist as students who graduate from high school. On the other hand, students who are expelled or who drop out for personal reasons having to do with marriage or pregnancy, or who leave school because of failing grades, are more likely to be delinquent than high-school graduates. Reasons, then, mediate the relationship between skipping or dropping out and delinquency.

SUMMARY

Critical criminologists' paramount concern is eliminating inequality in all realms of society. To do so, they struggle for fundamental social, political, and economic change, and advance short-term progressive policies. The main objective of this chapter was to discuss some contemporary critical criminological initiatives. Most of these proposals stem, in part, from the proposition that the criminal justice system is only one part of society and cannot be responsible all by itself for cleaning up the messes left by broader social forces (Currie, 1985). Throughout this book, it is repeatedly argued that social structural problems cause various types of crime and contribute to problematic and often destructive societal reactions to violations of legal norms.

There are, of course, many more initiatives that could be listed here and have been by others. The goal is for progressives from all walks of life to work closely together to promote the creation and maintenance of peaceful and equitable societies. Unfortunately, in the light of growing joblessness, massive cuts to social services, and other economic factors, "[t]he struggle to keep people focused on pushing for the necessary structural change is going to be more difficult" (Denham and Gillespie, 1999, p. 47). Nevertheless, if critical criminologists and other groups with similar goals do not stay focused and repeatedly promote progressive policies, many families, countries, and communities will continue to suffer from crime, social injustice, and a myriad of other major social problems. Perhaps, then, one of the best ways to conclude this chapter is to quote a section of Currie's (2008a, p. 117) commentary on the future of violence:

> The choice is stark and simple: We can either let that process continue and fortify ourselves against it, with more gated communities and more prisons, or we can decide that it is not tolerable and work to change it. What we cannot do is pretend that we don't know it's happening.

NOTES

1 Critical criminology: definition and brief history

1 Employment insurance (EI) offers temporary income for unem-ployed Canadians while they seek a job or try to upgrade their skills. EI also assists Canadians who are sick, pregnant, or who look after newborn or adopted children, as well as those who must care for a seriously ill family member at risk of dying (Service Canada, 2009).

2 Milton Friedman was born on July 31, 1912 and died on November 16, 2006. His (1962) book, *Capitalism and Freedom*, had a major impact on advocates of conservative and neo-conservative policies.

3 With the help of progressive organizations such as Legal Momentum, the American Civil Liberties Union, and the American Association of University Women, the plaintiffs appealed the dismissal and it was overturned in September 2007 (Fleury-Steiner and Miller, 2008; Simpson *v.* University of Colorado, Boulder, 2007). After that, the case was settled for approximately US$3 million, and the University of Colorado appointed an independent adviser on Title IX, sexual harassment, and sexual assault (Burnett and Vaughn, 2007).

4 This section includes revised versions of work published previously by DeKeseredy and Schwartz (1991a).

5 Administrative criminologists are often called right realists for their work in helping the state to administer the criminal justice system. James Q. Wilson in the United States and Ron Clarke, who did most of his work in the United Kingdom are two of the best-known administrative criminologists. Because their views tend to coincide more with the views of politicians, administrative criminologists have had a much greater impact on US and Canadian criminal justice policies than any other type of criminologist.

6 Some of the articles that appear in this issue were reprinted in James Incidari's (1980) controversial anthology, *Radical Criminology: The Coming Crises*.

7 This section includes modified sections of work published previously by DeKeseredy and Perry (2006a) and DeKeseredy and Schwartz (1996).

8 This sentence is derived from the title of MacLean and Milovanovic's (1997b) anthology, *Thinking Critically About Crime*.

2 Contemporary critical criminological schools of thought

1 As stated in Chapter 1, James Q. Wilson is an administrative criminologist and author of the widely read and cited conservative text, *Thinking About Crime* (1985).

2 This section includes revised versions of work published previously by DeKeseredy and Schwartz (1996, 2009).

3 Conducted in 1965, the Richmond Youth Project is a self-report survey of 4,075 Richmond, California high-school students.

4 A husband is exempt in these states if his wife is mentally ill or physically impaired, unconscious, asleep, or unable to consent (Bergen, 2006).

5 However, in all cases of wife beating where reasonable and probable grounds exist, charges are still not typical (DeKeseredy and Schwartz, 2009).

6 For example, see Messerschmidt (1993), Miller (1994), and Renzetti (1994).

7 For example, in the United States, between 50 percent and 90 percent of battered women try to leave abusive relationships (Block, 2003; DeKeseredy and Schwartz, 2009; Stark, 2007).

8 Parts of this section include revised sections of work published previously by DeKeseredy and Schwartz (2005a) and Schwartz and DeKeseredy (1997).

9 For example, evolutionary psychologists argue that male violence is the result of competition for sexual access to women. However, men kill not only men, but also women. See DeKeseredy and Schwartz (2005a), Kimmel (2000), and Polk (2003) for more criticisms of the evolutionary theory of male violence.

10 This section includes modified sections of work published previously by DeKeseredy (2007), DeKeseredy *et al.* (2006) and DeKeseredy and Schwartz (in press).

11 This section includes revised sections of work published previously by DeKeseredy and Schwartz (1996).

12 See Pepinsky and Quinney's (1991) edited book for essays giving more detailed descriptions of peacemaking criminology's intellectual, spiritual, philosophical, and political roots.

13 See Ptacek's (2010c) collection of essays on restorative justice and violence against women for more in-depth information on such feminist controversies.

14 This section includes modified sections of work published previously by DeKeseredy and Schwartz (1996).

15 Arguably, of all the European postmodern theorists, Michel Foucault has received the most attention in criminological circles. His (1977) book, *Discipline and Punish*, was especially influential (Schwartz and Friedrichs, 1994).

16 See, for example, his (2006) chapter in DeKeseredy and Perry's (2006c) anthology, *Advancing Critical Criminology*.

17 Presdee's (2000) *Cultural Criminology and the Carnival of Crime* is essential reading for those seeking a richer understanding of cultural criminology. The same can be said of Ferrell *et al.*'s (2008) book, *Cultural Criminology: An Invitation*.

18 This section includes modified sections of work published previously by DeKeseredy and Schwartz (in press).

3 Contemporary critical criminological research

1 See, for example, Donnermeyer, Kreps, and Kreps (1999) and Kreps, Donnermeyer, and Kreps (1997).

2 Edgework is defined as "acts of extreme voluntary risk taking" (Ferrell *et al.*, 2008, p. 72). Rather than being self-destructive, edgework is a means of reacting against the "unidentifiable forces that rob one of individual choice" (Lyng, 1990, p. 870).

3 This section includes slightly modified parts of work published previously by Donnermeyer and DeKeseredy (2008).

4 See, for example, his (1985) seminal book, *Confronting Crime: An American Challenge*.

5 This is the title of Frank Pearce's (1976) pathbreaking Marxist analysis of corporate and organized crime.

6 See Rigakos (2002, p. 5) for sources on these schools of thought.

7 Intelligarde International is a private law-enforcement company founded by Ross MacLeod who first developed the concept of parapolice.

8 This section includes modified sections of work published previously by DeKeseredy and Olsson (in press).

4 Confronting crime: critical criminological policies

1 This chapter includes modified sections of work published previously by DeKeseredy (2009a) and DeKeseredy and Schwartz (1996).

2 The Tackling Violent Crime Act includes the following revisions to the Canadian *Criminal Code*: automatically refusing bail to people charged with gun crimes; making it easier for police to charge people driving under the influence of drugs; raising the legal age of sexual consent to 16 from 14; making it easier to prosecute and indefinitely incarcerate "dangerous offenders" after three convictions for serious crimes; and mandatory minimum prison sentences for drug dealers.

3 The Russian Federation had the second highest incarceration rate in the world and the United States had the highest rate (700 per 100,000 population (Currie, 2008a; International Centre for Prison Studies, 2007)).

4 This section includes modified portions of work published previously by DeKeseredy (in press a) and DeKeseredy and Schwartz (1998).

5 For more information on the Clean Hotel Initiative, go to www.menaspeacemakers.org/programs/mnman/hotels.

6 See, for example, the 1975 Hollywood movie, *Jaws*.

7 This section includes revised sections of work published previously by DeKeseredy (2007) and DeKeseredy *et al.* (2005).

REFERENCES

Adler, P.A., and Adler, P. (Eds). (2003). *Constructions of deviance: Social power, context, and interaction* (4th ed.). Belmont, CA: Wadsworth.

Akers, R.L. (1997). *Criminological theories: Introduction and evaluation* (2nd ed.). Los Angeles, CA: Roxbury.

Akers, R.L., and Sellers, C.S. (2004). *Criminological theories: Introduction, evaluation, and application* (4th ed.). Los Angeles, CA: Roxbury.

Alvarez, A., and Bachman, R. (2008). *Violence: The enduring problem*. Thousand Oaks, CA: Sage.

Alvi, S., DeKeseredy, W.S., and Ellis, D. (2000). *Contemporary social problems in North American society*. Toronto, ON: Addison Wesley Longman.

Anderson, E. (2008). 'Against the wall: Poor, young, black, and male.' In E. Anderson (Ed.), *Against the wall: Poor, young, black, and male* (pp. 1–27). Philadelphia, PA: University of Pennsylvania Press.

Andrews, D.A., and Bonta, J. (2006). *The psychology of criminal conduct* (4th ed.). Cincinnati, OH: LexisNexis.

Arrigo, B.A. (2003). 'Postmodern justice and critical criminology: Positional, relational, and provisional justice.' In M.D. Schwartz and S.E. Hatty (Eds.), *Controversies in critical criminology* (pp. 43–56). Cincinnati, ON: Anderson Publishing.

Austin, J., and Coventry, G. (2001). *Emerging issues on privatized prisons*. Washington, DC: National Institute of Justice.

Barak, G. (1986). 'Is America really ready for the Currie challenge?' *Crime and Social Justice, 25*, 200–203.

Barak, G. (1988). 'Newsmaking criminology: Reflections on the media, intellectuals, and crime.' *Justice Quarterly, 5*, 565–588.

Barak, G. (Ed.). (1991). *Crimes by the capitalist state: An introduction to state criminality*. Albany, NY: SUNY Press.

Barak, G. (1995a). 'Time for an integrated criminology.' *The Critical Criminologist, 7*, 3–6.

Barak, G. (Ed.). (1995b). *Media, process, and the social construction of crime: Studies in newsmaking criminology*. New York, NY: Garland.

Barker, J. (2009). 'A "typical" female offender.' In J. Barker (Ed.), *Women and the criminal justice system: A Canadian perspective* (pp. 63–88). Toronto, ON: Emond Montgomery.

Barrett, M. (1985). *Women's oppression today: Problems in Marxist feminist analysis.* London: Verso.

Barrett, M., and McIntosh, M. (1982). *The anti-social family.* London: Verso.

Basran, G.S., Gill, C., and MacLean, B.D. (1995). *Farmworkers and their children.* Vancouver, BC: Collective Press.

Becker, H.S. (1967). 'Whose side are we on?' *Social Problems, 14,* 239–247.

Becker, H.S. (1973). *Outsiders: Studies in the sociology of deviance.* New York: Free Press.

Bergen, R.K. (2006). 'Marital rape: New research and directions.' *VAWnet,* February, 1–13.

Belknap, J. (2005, November). 'What I saw at the Title IX revolution: University charged as a rape training institution.' Paper presented at the American Society of Criminology meetings, Toronto, Canada.

Best, J. (1990). *Threatened children: Rhetoric and concern about child victims.* Chicago, IL: University of Chicago Press.

Blau, J., and Blau, P. (1982). 'The cost of inequality: Metropolitan structure and violent crime.' *American Sociological Review, 47,* 114–129.

Block, C.R. (2003). 'How can practitioners help an abused woman lower her risk of death.' *NIJ Journal, 250,* 4–7.

Boehringer, G., Brown, D., Edgeworth, B., Hogg, R., and Ramsey, I. (1983). 'Law and order for progressives? An Australian response.' *Crime and Social Justice, 25,* 200–203.

Bourgois, P. (1995). *In search of respect: Selling crack in El Barrio.* New York, NY: Cambridge University Press.

Bowker, L. (1983). *Beating wife beating.* Lexington, MA: Lexington Books.

Box, S. (1983). *Power, crime and mystification.* London: Tavistock.

Braithwaite, J. (1984). *Corporate crime in the pharmaceutical industry.* London: Routledge and Kegan Paul.

Browne, I. (1997). 'The black–white gap in labor force participation among women.' *American Sociological Review, 62,* 236–252.

Brownstein, H. (1991). 'The social construction of public policy.' *Sociological Practice Review, 2,* 132–140.

Bureau of Labor Statistics. (2009). 'Summer youth labor force release.' Washington, DC: US Department of Labor.

Burnett, S., and Vaughn, K. (2007, December 6). 'CU makes $2.85M vow for change: Barnett responds.' *Rocky Mountain News.*

Retrieved May 23, 2008, from www.rockymountainnews.com/news/2007/dec/06/sex-assault-suit-settled.

Caputo, G.A. (2008). *Out in the storm: Drug-addicted women living as shoplifters and sex workers.* Boston, MA: Northeastern University Press.

Carastathis, A. (2006, October 11). 'New cuts and conditions for Status of Women Canada.' *Toronto Star.* Retrieved October 11, 2006, from www.dominionpaper.ca/canadian_news/2006/10/11new_cuts_a.html.

Caringella-MacDonald, S., and Humphries, D. (1998). 'Guest editors' introduction.' *Violence Against Women, 4*, 3–9.

Carrington, K., and Hogg, R. (2008). 'Critical criminologies: An introduction.' In K. Carrington and R. Hogg (Eds), *Critical criminology: Issues, debates, challenges* (pp. 1–12). Portland, OR: Willan.

Chakraborti, N., and Garland, J. (Eds). (2004). *Rural racism.* Portland, OR: Willan.

Chambliss, W. (1975). 'Toward a political economy of crime.' *Theory and Society*, Summer, 167–180.

Chambliss, W. (1986). 'On lawmaking.' In S. Brickey and E. Comack (Eds), *The social basis of law: Critical readings in the sociology of law* (pp. 27–51). Toronto, ON: Garamond.

Chambliss, W., and Seidman, R. (1982). *Law, order, and power* (2nd ed.). Reading, MA: Addison-Wesley.

Chermak, S., Bailey, F.Y., and Brown, M. (2003). 'Introduction.' In S. Chermak, F.Y. Bailey, and M. Brown (Eds), *Media representations of September 11* (pp. 1–14). Westport, CT: Praeger.

Chesney-Lind, M. (2001). 'Girls, violence and delinquency.' In S.O. White (Ed.), *Handbook of youth and justice* (pp. 135–158). New York, NY: Kluwer Academic/Plenum.

Chesney-Lind, M. (2007). 'Epilogue: Criminal justice, gender and diversity – A call for passion and public criminology.' In S.L. Miller (Ed.), *Criminal justice research and practice: Diverse voices in the field* (pp. 210–220). Boston, MA: Northeastern University Press.

Chesney-Lind, M., and Irwin, K. (2008). *Beyond bad girls: Gender, violence and hype.* New York, NY: Routledge.

Chesney-Lind, M., and Pasko, L. (2004). *The female offender: Girls, women, and crime* (2nd ed.). Thousand Oaks, CA: Sage.

Clear, T.R. (2007). *Imprisoning communities: How mass incarceration makes disadvantaged neighborhoods worse.* New York, NY: Oxford University Press.

Cloward, R.A., and Ohlin, L.E. (1960). *Delinquency and opportunity: A theory of delinquent gangs.* New York, NY: Free Press of Glencoe.

Cohen, A. (1955). *Delinquent boys: The culture of the gang*. New York, NY: Free Press.

Cohen, S. (1980). *Folk devils and moral panics*. Oxford: Basil Blackwell.

Cohen, S. (1981). 'Footprints in the sand.' In M. Fitzgerald, G. McLennan, and J. Pawson (Eds), *Crime and society* (pp. 183–206). London: Routledge and Kegan Paul.

Cohen, S. (1985). *Visions of social control*. London: Wiley-Blackwell.

Collins, P.H. (2000). *Black feminist thought* (2nd ed.). New York, NY: Routledge.

Connell, R.W. (1987). *Gender and power*. Stanford, CA: Stanford University Press.

Connell, R.W. (1995). *Masculinities*. Berkeley, CA: University of California Press.

Connell, R.W. (2000). 'Masculinity and violence in world perspective?' In A. Godenzi (Ed.), *Frieden, kultur und geschlecht* (pp. 65–84). Fribourg: University of Fribourg Press.

Connell, R.W., and Messerschmidt, J.W. (2005). 'Hegemonic masculinity: Rethinking the concept.' *Gender and Society, 19*, 829–859.

Corsianos, M. (2009). *Policing and gendered justice: Examining the possibilities*. Toronto, ON: University of Toronto Press.

Courtwright, K.E., Mackey, D.A., and Packard, S.H. (2005). 'Empathy among college students and criminal justice majors.' *Journal of Criminal Justice Education, 16*, 125–144.

Crawford, A., Jones, T., Woodhouse, T., and Young, J. (1990). *Second Islington crime survey*. Middlesex: Centre for Criminology, Middlesex Polytechnic.

Crespo, M. (1987). 'The school skipper.' In E. Rubington and M.S. Weinberg (Eds), *Deviance: The interactionist perspective* (pp. 307–314). New York, NY: Macmillan.

Curran, D.J., and Renzetti, C.M. (1994). *Theories of crime*. Boston, MA: Allyn and Bacon.

Curran, D.J., and Renzetti, C.M. (2001). *Theories of crime* (2nd ed.). Boston, MA: Allyn and Bacon.

Currie, D.H., and MacLean, B.D. (1993). 'Preface.' In D.H. Currie and B.D. MacLean (Eds), *Social inequality, social justice* (pp. 5–6). Vancouver, BC: Collective Press.

Currie, E. (1985). *Confronting crime: An American challenge*. New York, NY: Pantheon.

Currie, E. (1992). 'Retreatism, minimalism, realism: Three styles of reasoning on crime and drugs in the United States.' In J. Lowman and B.D. MacLean (Eds), *Realist criminology: Crime control and policing in the 1990s* (pp. 88–97). Toronto, ON: University of Toronto Press.

Currie, E. (1993). *Reckoning: Drugs, the cities and the American future*. New York, NY: Hill and Wang.

Currie, E. (2004). *The road to whatever: Middle-class culture and the crisis of adolescence*. New York, NY: Metropolitan Books.

Currie, E. (2007). 'Against marginality: Arguments for a public criminology.' *Theoretical Criminology, 11*, 175–190.

Currie, E. (2008a). *The roots of danger: Violent crime in global perspective*. Upper Saddle River, NJ: Prentice Hall.

Currie, E. (2008b). 'Preface.' In K. Carrington and R. Hogg (Eds), *Critical criminology: Issues, debates, challenges* (pp. vii–ix). Portland, OR: Willan.

Daly, K., and Chesney-Lind, M. (1988). 'Feminism and criminology.' *Justice Quarterly, 5*, 497–538.

Daly, M., and Wilson, M. (1988). *Homicide*. Hawthorne, NY: Aldine de Gruyter.

Daniels, J. (2009). *Cyber racism: White supremacy online and the new attack on civil rights*. Lanham, MD: Roman and Littlefield.

Davidson, J.T., and Chesney-Lind, M. (2009). 'Discounting women: Context matters in risk and need assessment.' *Critical Criminology, 17*, 221–246.

De Giorgi, A. (2008). 'Rethinking the political economy of punishment.' *Criminal Justice Matters, 70*, 17–18.

DeGue, S., and DiLillo, D. (2008). 'Is animal cruelty a "red flag" for family violence? Investigating co-occurring violence toward children, partners, and pets.' *Journal of Interpersonal Violence, 24*, 1036–1056.

de Hann, W. (2009). 'Abolitionism and crime control.' In T. Newburn (Ed.), *Key readings in criminology* (pp. 21–274). Portland, OR: Willan.

DeKeseredy, W.S. (1990). 'Male peer support and woman abuse: The current stake of knowledge.' *Sociological Focus, 23*, 129–139.

DeKeseredy, W.S. (2007). 'Review of Elliott Currie's *The Road to Whatever: Middle-class Culture and the Crisis of Adolescence*.' *Critical Criminology, 15*, 199–201.

DeKeseredy, W.S. (2009a). 'Canadian crime control in the new millennium: The influence of neo-conservative policies and practices.' *Police Practice and Research, 10*, 305–316.

DeKeseredy, W.S. (2009b). 'Male violence against women in North America as hate crime.' In B. Perry (Ed.), *Hate crimes volume 3: The victims of hate crime* (pp. 151–172). Santa Barbara, CA: Praeger.

DeKeseredy, W.S. (2009c). 'Patterns of violence in the family.' In M. Baker (Ed.), *Families: Changing trends in Canada* (6th ed.) (pp. 179–205). Whitby, ON: McGraw-Hill Ryerson.

DeKeseredy, W.S. (in press a). *Violence against women in Canada.* Toronto, ON: University of Toronto Press.

DeKeseredy, W.S. (in press b). 'Bourgois, Phillipe: In search of respect.' In F.T. Cullen and P. Wilcox (Eds), *Encyclopedia of criminological theory.* Thousand Oaks, CA: Sage.

DeKeseredy, W.S., Alvi, S., and Schwartz, M.D. (2006). 'Left realism revisited.' In W.S. DeKeseredy and B. Perry (Eds), *Advancing critical criminology: Theory and application* (pp. 19–42). Lanham, MD: Lexington Books.

DeKeseredy, W.S., Alvi, S., Schwartz, M.D., and Tomaszewski, E.A. (2003). *Under siege: Poverty and crime in a public housing community.* Lanham, MD: Lexington Books.

DeKeseredy, W.S., Donnermeyer, J.F., Schwartz, M.D., Tunnell, K.D., and Hall, M. (2007a). 'Thinking critically about rural gender relations: Toward a rural masculinity crisis/male peer support model of separation/divorce sexual assault.' *Critical Criminology, 15,* 295–311.

DeKeseredy, W.S., and Dragiewicz, M. (2007). 'Understanding the complexities of feminist perspectives on woman abuse: A commentary on Donald G. Dutton's *Rethinking Domestic Violence.*' *Violence Against Women, 13,* 874–884.

DeKeseredy, W.S., Ellis, D., and Alvi, S. (2005). *Deviance and crime: Theory, research and policy.* Cincinnati, OH: Anderson Publishing.

DeKeseredy, W.S., and Goff, C. (1992). 'Corporate violence against Canadian women: Assessing left-realist research and policy.' *Journal of Human Justice, 4,* 55–70.

DeKeseredy, W.S., and Hinch, R. (1991). *Woman abuse: Sociological perspectives.* Toronto, ON: Thompson Educational Publishing.

DeKeseredy, W.S., and Joseph, C. (2006). 'Separation/divorce sexual assault in rural Ohio: Preliminary results of an exploratory study.' *Violence Against Women, 12,* 301–311.

DeKeseredy, W.S., and Olsson, P. (in press). 'Adult pornography, male peer support, and violence against women: The contribution of the "dark side" of the internet.' In M. Varga Martin and M.A. Garcia-Ruiz (Eds), *Technology for facilitating humanity and combating social deviations: Interdisciplinary perspectives.* Hershey, PA: IGI Global.

DeKeseredy, W.S., and Perry, B. (2006a). 'Introduction: The never-ending and constantly evolving journey.' In W.S. DeKeseredy and B. Perry (Eds), *Advancing critical criminology: Theory and application* (pp. 1–8). Lanham, MD: Lexington Books.

DeKeseredy, W.S., and Perry, B. (2006b). 'Introduction to part I.' In W.S. DeKeseredy and B. Perry (Eds), *Advancing critical criminology: Theory and application* (pp. 11–17). Lanham, MD: Lexington Books.

DeKeseredy, W.S., and Perry, B. (Eds). (2006c). *Advancing critical criminology: Theory and application*. Lanham, MD: Lexington Books.

DeKeseredy, W.S., Perry, B., and Schwartz, M.D. (2007). 'Hate-motivated sexual assault on the college campus: Results from a Canadian representative sample.' Paper presented at the annual meeting of the American Society of Criminology, Atlanta.

DeKeseredy, W.S., and Schwartz, M.D. (1991a). 'British and U.S. left realism: A critical comparison.' *International Journal of Offender Therapy and Comparative Criminology*, 35, 248–262.

DeKeseredy, W.S., and Schwartz, M.D. (1991b). 'British left realism on the abuse of women: A critical appraisal.' In H. Pepinsky and R. Quinney (Eds), *Criminology as peacemaking* (pp. 154–171). Bloomington, IN: Indiana University Press.

DeKeseredy, W.S., and Schwartz, M.D. (1993). 'Male peer support and woman abuse: An expansion of DeKeseredy's model.' *Sociological Spectrum, 13*, 394–414.

DeKeseredy, W.S., and Schwartz, M.D. (1996). *Contemporary criminology*. Belmont, CA: Wadsworth.

DeKeseredy, W.S., and Schwartz, M.D. (1998). *Woman abuse on campus: Results from the Canadian national survey*. Thousand Oaks, CA: Sage.

DeKeseredy, W.S., and Schwartz, M.D. (2002). 'Theorizing public housing woman abuse as a function of economic exclusion and male peer support.' *Women's Health and Urban Life, 1*, 26–45.

DeKeseredy, W.S., and Schwartz, M.D. (2005a). 'Masculinities and interpersonal violence.' In M.S. Kimmel, J. Hearn, and R.W. Connell (Eds), *Handbook of studies on men and masculinities* (pp. 353–366). Thousand Oaks, CA: Sage.

DeKeseredy, W.S., and Schwartz, M.D. (2005b). 'Left realist theory.' In S. Henry and M. Lanier (Eds), *The essential criminology reader*. Boulder, CA: Westview Press.

DeKeseredy, W.S., and Schwartz, M.D. (2009). *Dangerous exits: Escaping abusive relationships in rural America*. New Brunswick, NJ: Rutgers University Press.

DeKeseredy, W.S., and Schwartz, M.D. (in press). 'Friedman economic policies, social exclusion, and crime: Toward a gendered left realist subcultural theory.' *Crime, Law and Social Change*.

DeKeseredy, W.S., Schwartz, M.D., Fagen, D., and Hall, M. (2006). 'Separation/divorce sexual assault: The contribution of male peer support.' *Feminist Criminology, 1*, 228–250.

Delacourt, S. (2009, October 26). 'Tory heckles drown out Liberal MP's flu questions.' *Toronto Star*, p. A8.

Denham, D., and Gillespie, J. (1999). *Two steps forward ... one step back*. Ottawa, ON: Health Canada.

Denzin, N. (1990). 'Presidential address on the sociological imagination revisited.' *The Sociological Quarterly, 31*, 1–22.

Devine, J.A., and Wright, J.D. (1993). *The greatest of evils: Urban poverty and the American underclass*. New York, NY: Aldine de Gruyter.

Dews, P. (1987). *Logic of disintegration: Poststructuralist thought and claims of critical thought*. New York, NY: Verso.

Dines, G. (2006). 'The white man's burden: Gonzo pornography and the construction of black masculinity.' *Yale Journal of Law and Feminism, 18*, 296–297.

Dines, G., and Jensen, R. (2008a). 'Pornography.' In C.M. Renzetti and J.L. Edleson (Eds), *Encyclopedia of interpersonal violence* (pp. 519–520). Thousand Oaks, CA: Sage.

Dines, G., and Jensen, R. (2008b). 'Internet, pornography.' In C.M. Renzetti and J.L. Edleson (Eds), *Encyclopedia of interpersonal violence* (pp. 365–366). Thousand Oaks, CA: Sage.

Dobash, R.E., and Dobash, R. (1979). *Violence against wives: A case against the patriarchy*. New York, NY: Free Press.

Donnermeyer, J.F. (2007). 'Rural crime: Roots and restoration.' *International Journal of Rural Crime, 1*, 2–20.

Donnermeyer, J.F., and DeKeseredy, W.S. (2008). 'Toward a rural critical criminology.' *Southern Rural Sociology, 23*, 4–28.

Donnermeyer, J.F., DeKeseredy, W.S., and Dragiewicz, M. (in press). 'Policing rural Canada and the United States.' In R. Yarwood and R. Mawby (Eds), *Countryside constable*. Aldershot: Ashgate.

Donnermeyer, J.F., Jobes, P., and Barclay, E. (2006). 'Rural crime, poverty, and community.' In W.S. DeKeseredy and B. Perry (Eds), *Advancing critical criminology: Theory and application* (pp. 199–218). Lanham, MD: Lexington Books.

Donnermeyer, J.F., Kreps, G.M., and Kreps, M.W. (1999). *Lessons for living: A practical approach to daily life from the Amish community*. Sugarcreek, OH: Carlisle Press.

Dragiewicz, M. (2009). 'Why sex and gender matter in domestic violence research and advocacy.' In E. Stark and E.S. Buzawa (Eds), *Violence against women in families and relationships, volume 3: Criminal justice and the law* (pp. 201–216). Santa Barbara, CA: Praeger.

Dragiewicz, M., and DeKeseredy, W.S. (2008). *A needs gap assessment report on abused women without legal representation in the family courts*. Oshawa, ON: Report prepared for Luke's Place Support and Resource Centre.

Dutton, D.G. (2006). *Rethinking domestic violence*. Vancouver, BC: University of British Columbia Press.

Dworkin, A. (1994). 'Pornography happens to women.' Retrieved August 15, 2009 from www.nostatusquo.com/ACLU/dworkin/Porn-Happens.html.

Ehrenreich, B. (2001). *Nickel and dimed: On (not) getting by in America*. New York, NY: Metropolitan Books.

Ehrlich, H.J. (1999). 'Campus ethnoviolence.' In F. Pincus and H.J. Ehrlich (Eds), *Ethnic conflict* (pp. 277–290). Boulder, CO: Westview.

Eisenstein, Z. (1980). *Capitalist patriarchy and the case for socialist feminism*. New York, NY: Monthly Review Press.

Elias, R. (1986). *The politics of victimization*. New York, NY: Oxford University Press.

Ellis, D. (1987). *The wrong stuff: An introduction to the sociological study of deviance*. Toronto, ON: Macmillan.

Ellis, D., and DeKeseredy, W.S. (1996). *The wrong stuff: An introduction to the sociological study of deviance* (2nd ed.). Toronto, ON: Allyn and Bacon.

Ferrell, J. (1994). 'Confronting the agenda of authority: Critical criminology, anarchism and urban graffiti.' In G. Barak (Ed.), *Varieties of criminology* (pp. 161–178). New York, NY: Praeger.

Ferrell, J. (1995) 'Culture, crime and cultural criminology.' *Journal of Criminal Justice and Popular Culture, 3*, 25–42.

Ferrell, J. (1998). 'Stumbling toward a critical criminology (and into the anarchy and imagery of postmodernism).' In J.I. Ross (Ed.), *Cutting the edge* (pp. 63–76). Westport, CT: Praeger.

Ferrell, J. (2003). *Cultural criminology*. In M.D. Schwartz and S.E. Hatty (Eds), *Controversies in critical criminology* (pp. 71–84). Cincinnati, OH: Anderson Publishing.

Ferrell, J. (2006). *Empire of scrounge*. New York, NY: New York University Press.

Ferrell, J., Hayward, K., and Young, J. (2008). *Cultural criminology: An invitation*. London: Sage.

Ferrell, J., and Sanders, C. (Eds). (1995). *Cultural criminology*. Boston, MA: Northeastern University Press.

Fleury-Steiner, R.E., and S.L. Miller. (2008). 'Research, dissemination, and activism: Guest editors' introduction.' *Feminist Criminology, 3*, 243–246.

Foster, H., and Hagan, J. (2007). 'Incarceration and intergenerational social exclusion.' *Social Problems, 54*, 399–433.

Foucault, M. (1979). *Discipline and punish: The birth of the prison*. New York, NY: Vintage.

Friedman, M. (1962). *Capitalism and freedom*. Chicago, IL: University of Chicago Press.

Friedrichs, D.O. (1989). 'Critical criminology and critical legal studies.' *Critical Criminologist, 1*, 7.

Friedrichs, D.O. (1991). 'Introduction: Peacemaking criminology in a world filled with conflict.' In B. MacLean and D. Milovanovic (Eds), *New directions in critical criminology* (pp. 101–106). Vancouver, BC: Collective Press.

Friedrichs, D.O. (1996). 'Critical criminology: Strength in diversity for these times.' *Critical Criminology, 7*, 121–128.

Friedrichs, D.O. (2000). 'The crime of the century? The case for the holocaust.' *Crime, Law and Social Change, 34*, 21–41.

Friedrichs, D.O. (2001). *Law in our lives: An introduction*. Los Angeles, CA: Roxbury.

Friedrichs, D.O. (2007). *Trusted criminals: White collar crime in contemporary society* (3rd ed.). Belmont, CA: Wadsworth.

Friedrichs, D.O. (2009). 'Critical criminology.' In J.M. Miller (Ed.), *21st century criminology: A reference handbook, volume 1* (pp. 210–218). Thousand Oaks, CA: Sage.

Fuller, J.R., and Wozniak, J.F. (2006). 'Peacemaking criminology: Past, present, and future.' In F.T. Cullen, J.P. Wright, and K.B. Blevins (Eds), *Taking stock: The status of criminological theory* (pp. 251–273). New Brunswick, NJ: Transaction Publishing.

Funk, R.E. (2006). *Reaching men: Strategies for preventing sexist attitudes, behaviors, and violence*. Indianapolis, IN: Jist Life.

Gabbidon, S.L., and Greene, H.T. (2005). *Race and crime*. Thousand Oaks, CA: Sage.

Galt, V. (2009, August 7). 'Youth bear brunt of job losses: Canada's student unemployment rate hits almost 21 percent in July, the highest on record.' *Globe and Mail*, p. 1.

Garbarino, J. (2006). *See Jane hit: Why girls are growing more violent and what we can do about it*. New York, NY: Penguin Press.

Garcia-Moreno, C., Jansen, A.F.M.H., Ellsberg, M., Heise, L., and Watts, C. (2005). *WHO multi-country study on women's health and domestic violence against women: Initial results on prevalence, health outcomes, and women's responses*. Geneva: World Health Organization.

Gardiner, J.K. (2005). 'Men, masculinities, and feminist theory.' In M.S. Kimmel, J. Hearn, and R.W. Connell (Eds), *Handbook of studies on men and masculinities* (pp. 35–50). Thousand Oaks, CA: Sage.

Gelsthorpe, L., and Morris, A. (1988). 'Feminism and criminology in Britain.' *British Journal of Criminology, 28*, 93–110.

Gibbons, D. (1994). *Talking about crime and criminals: Problems and issues in theory development in criminology.* Englewood Cliffs, NJ: Prentice Hall.

Gibbons, D. (1995). 'Unfit for human consumption: The problem of flawed writing in criminal justice and what to do about it.' *Crime and Delinquency, 41*, 246–266.

Gibbs, J.C. (in press). 'Looking at terrorism through left realist lenses.' *Crime, Law and Social Change.*

Giordano, P.C. (1995). 'The wider circle of friends in adolescence.' *American Journal of Sociology, 101*, 661–97.

Goel, R. (2010). 'Aboriginal women and political pursuit in Canadian sentencing circles: At cross roads or cross purposes?' In J. Ptacek (Ed.), *Restorative justice and violence against women* (pp. 60–78). New York, NY: Oxford University Press.

Goff, C., and Reasons, C. (1978). *Corporate crime in Canada.* Scarborough, ON: Prentice-Hall.

Goodwin, G. (1983). 'Toward a paradigm for humanist sociology.' *Humanity and Society, 7*, 219–237.

Grant, J. (1993). *Fundamental feminism: Contesting the core concepts of feminist theory.* New York, NY: Routledge.

Grant, J. (2008). *Charting women's journeys: From addiction to recovery.* Lanham, MD: Lexington Books.

Griffiths, C.T. (2007). *Canadian criminal justice: A primer* (3rd ed.). Toronto, ON: Thomson.

Hagan, J. (1985). 'The assumption of natural science methods: Criminological positivism.' In R.F. Meir (Ed.), *Theoretical methods in criminology* (pp. 75–92). Beverly Hills, CA: Sage.

Hagedorn, J.M. (1988). *People and folks: Gangs, crime and the underclass in a rustbelt city.* Chicago, IL: Lakeview Press.

Hall, S., Critcher, C., Jefferson, T., Clarke, J., and Roberts, B. (1978). *Policing the crisis: Mugging, the state, and law and order.* London: Macmillan.

Harding, S. (1987). 'Is there a feminist method?' In S. Harding (Ed.), *Feminism and methodology* (pp. 1–14). Bloomington, IN: Indiana University Press.

Harvey, L. (1990). *Critical social research.* London: Unwin Hyman.

Hatty, S.E. (2000). *Masculinities, violence, and culture.* Thousand Oaks, CA: Sage.

Hayward, K. (2007). 'Cultural criminology.' In B. Goldson (Ed.), *The dictionary of youth justice* (pp. 119–120). Cullompton: Willan.

Hayward, K., and Young, J. (2004). 'Cultural criminology: Some notes on the script.' *Theoretical Criminology, 8*, 250–273.

Hebert, C. (2007, October 19). 'Dion now looks down the barrel.' *Toronto Star*, A17.

Hebert, C. (2010, January 15). 'Court of public opinion turns on Tories.' *Toronto Star*. Retreived January 20, 2010, from www.thestar.com/news/canada/article/751087-hebert-court-of-public-opinion-turns-on-tories.

Heilbroner, R. (1980). *Marxism, for and against*. New York, NY: Norton.

Helmkamp, J., Ball, J., and Townsend, K. (Eds). (1996). *Definitional dilemma: Can and should there be a universal definition of white collar crime?* Morgantown, WV: National White Collar Crime Center.

Henry, S. (1999). 'Is Left realism a useful theory for addressing the problems of crime? No.' In J.R. Fuller and E.W. Hickey (Eds), *Controversial issues in criminology* (pp. 137–144). Boston, MA: Allyn and Bacon.

Henry, S., and Milovanovic, D. (1993). 'Back to basics: A postmodern redefinition of crime.' *The Critical Criminologist*, 5(1–2), 12.

Henry, S., and Milovanovic, D. (2003). 'Constitutive criminology.' In M.D. Schwartz and S.E. Hatty (Eds), *Controversies in critical criminology* (pp. 57–70). Cincinnati, OH: Anderson Publishing.

Henry, S., and Milovanovic, D. (2005). 'Postmodernism and constitutive theories of criminal behavior.' In R.A. Wright and J.M. Miller (Eds), *Encyclopedia of criminology, volume 2* (pp. 1245–1249). New York, NY: Routledge.

Hirschi, T. (1969). *Causes of delinquency*. Berkeley, CA: University of California Press.

Hogg, R., and Carrington, K. (2006). *Policing the rural crisis*. Sydney: Federation Press.

Hornqvist, M. (2008). 'Prison expansion without a labour market orientation.' *Criminal Justice Matters*, 70, 19–20.

Hottocks, R. (1994). *Masculinity in crisis*. New York, NY: St. Martin's Press.

Housing Assistance Council. (2002). *Taking stock of rural people, poverty, and housing for the 21st century*. Washington, DC: Author.

Human Rights Watch (2008). *Targeting blacks*. New York, NY: Author.

Hunnicutt, G. (2009). 'Varieties of patriarchy and violence against women: Resurrecting "patriarchy" as a theoretical tool.' *Violence Against Women*, 15, 553–573.

Inciardi, J.A. (Ed.). (1980). *Radical criminology: The coming crises*. Beverly Hills, CA: Sage.

International Center for Prison Studies. (2007). *World prison brief.* Retrieved September 11, 2009, from http://www.kcl.ac.uk/depsta/rel/icps/worldbrief.

Iovanni, L., and Miller, S.L. (2001). 'Criminal justice system responses to domestic violence: Law enforcement and the courts.' In C.M. Renzetti, J.L. Edleson, and R.K. Bergen (Eds), *Sourcebook on violence against women* (pp. 303–328). Thousand Oaks, CA: Sage.

Irwin, J., and Austin, J. (1994). *It's about time: America's imprisonment binge.* Belmont, CA: Sage.

Jacobs, J. (2004). *Dark age ahead.* Toronto, ON: Vintage.

Jarjoura, G.R. (1993). 'Does dropping out of school enhance delinquent involvement? Results from a large scale national probability sample.' *Criminology, 31,* 149–170.

Jensen, R. (2007). *Getting off: Pornography and the end of masculinity.* Cambridge, MA: South End Press.

Jensen, R., and Dines, G. (1998). 'The content of mass-marketed pornography.' In G. Dines, R. Jensen, and A. Russo (Eds), *Pornography: The production and consumption of inequality* (pp. 65–100). New York, NY: Routledge.

Jobes, P.C., Barclay, E., Weinand, H., and Donnermeyer, J.F. (2004). 'A structural analysis of social disorganization and crime in rural communities in Australia.' *The Australian and New Zealand Journal of Criminology, 37,* 114–140.

Johnson, H. (1996). *Dangerous domains: Violence against women in Canada.* Toronto, ON: Nelson.

Johnson, H., Ollus, N., and Nevala, S. (2008). *Violence against women: An international perspective.* New York, NY: Springer.

Jones, N. (2010). *Between good and ghetto: African American girls and inner-city violence.* New Brunswick, NJ: Rutgers University Press.

Katz, J., and Chambliss, W.J. (1991). 'Biology and crime.' In J.F. Sheley (Ed.), *Criminology: A contemporary handbook* (pp. 245–271). Belmont, CA: Wadsworth.

Katz, L. (1978). 'Work: It's more dangerous for public employees.' *The Public Employee, 1,* 6.

Kauzlarich, D. (2006). 'Foreword.' In D. Rothe and C.W. Mullins, *Symbolic gestures and the generation of global social control: The International Criminal Court.* Lanham, MD: Lexington Books.

Kauzlarich, D., and Matthews, R.A. (2006). 'Taking stock of theory and research.' In R.J. Michalowski and R.C. Kramer (Eds), *State–corporate crime: Wrongdoing at the intersection of business and government* (pp. 239–250). New Brunswick, NJ: Rutgers University Press.

Kelling, G., and Coles, C. (1997). *Fixing broken windows*. New York, NY: Free Press.

Kimmel, M.S. (2000). *The gendered society*. New York, NY: Oxford University Press.

Kinsey, R., Lea, J., and Young, J. (1986). *Losing the fight against crime*. Oxford: Blackwell.

Klein, M.W. (2007). *Chasing after street gangs: A forty-year journey*. Upper Saddle River, NJ: Prentice Hall.

Klein, N. (2007). *The shock doctrine: The rise of disaster capitalism*. Toronto, ON: Knopf.

Kramer, R.C. (2006). 'The space shuttle challenger explosion.' In R.J. Michalowski and R.C. Kramer (Eds), *State–corporate crime: Wrongdoing at the intersection of business and government* (pp. 27–44). New Brunswick, NJ: Rutgers University Press.

Kramer, R.C., Michalowski, R., and Kauzlarich, D. (2002). 'The origins and development of the concept and theory of state–corporate crime.' *Crime and Delinquency, 48*, 263–282.

Kreps, G.M., Donnermeyer, J.F., and Kreps, M.W. (1997). *A quiet moment in time*. Sugar Creek, OH: Carlisle Press.

Krug, E., Dahlberg, E.L., and Mercy, J. *et al.* (2002). *World report on violence and health*. Geneva: World Health Organization.

Kubrin, C., Stucky, T.D., and Krohn, M.D. (2009). *Researching theories of crime and deviance*. New York, NY: Oxford University Press.

Lea, J., and Young, J. (1984). *What is to be done about law and order?* New York, NY: Penguin.

Legislative Analyst's Office. (2010). 'Analysis of the California 2008–09 budget bill: Criminal justice.' Retrieved January 27, 2010, from www.lao.ca.gov/analysis_2008/crim_justice/cj_anl08008.aspx.

Lemert, E.M. (1951). *Social pathology*. New York, NY: McGraw-Hill.

Leonard, K. (1974). 'Progressive professors on thin ice here and nationwide.' *New University, 6*(1), 16.

Lewin, K. (1951). *Field theory in social science: Selected theoretical papers*. New York, NY: Harper and Row.

Lewis, O. (1966). *La Vida: A Puerto Rican family in the culture of poverty – San Juan and New York*. New York, NY: Random House.

Li, G. (2007). 'Homicide in Canada, 2006.' *Juristat: Canadian Centre for Justice Statistics, 27*, 1–19.

Liazos, A. (1972). 'The poverty of the sociology of deviance: Nuts, sluts and perverts.' *Social Problems, 20*, 103–120.

Lilly, J.R., Cullen, F.T., and Ball, R.A. (2007). *Criminological theory: Context and consequences* (4th ed.). Thousand Oaks, CA: Sage.

Liska, A.E. (1987). 'A critical examination of macro perspectives on crime control.' *Annual Review of Sociology, 13,* 67–88.

Longino, H. (1980). 'What is pornography?' In L. Lederer (Ed.), *Take back the night: Women on pornography* (pp. 40–54). New York, NY: William Morrow.

Luttwak, E. (1995, November). 'Turbo-charged capitalism and its consequences.' *London Review of Books,* pp. 6–7.

Lynch, M.J., Michalowski, R., and Groves, W.B. (2000). *The new primer in radical criminology: Critical perspectives on crime, power and identity* (3rd ed.). Monsey, NJ: Criminal Justice Press.

Lynch, M.J., and Stretesky, P. (2001). 'Toxic crimes: Examining corporate victimization of the general public employing medical and epidemiological evidence.' *Critical Criminology, 10,* 153–172.

Lyng, S. (1990). 'Edgework.' *American Journal of Sociology, 95,* 851–856.

Lyng, S. (Ed.). (2005). *Edgework.* New York, NY: Routledge.

MacLean, B.D. (1991). 'In partial defense of socialist realism: Some theoretical and methodological concerns of the local crime survey.' *Crime, Law and Social Change, 15,* 213–254.

MacLean, B.D., and Milovanovic, D. (1997a). 'Thinking critically about criminology.' In B.D. MacLean and D. Milovanovic (Eds), *Thinking critically about crime* (pp. 1–16). Vancouver, BC: Collective Press.

MacLean, B.D., and Milovanovic, D. (Eds). (1997b). *Thinking critically about crime.* Vancouver, BC: Collective Press.

Maidment, M.R. (2006). 'Transgressing boundaries: Feminist perspectives in criminology.' In W.S. DeKeseredy and B. Perry (Eds), *Advancing critical criminology: Theory and application* (pp. 43–62). Lanham, MD: Lexington Books.

Manning, P.K. (1997). *Police work: The social organization of policing* (2nd ed.). Prospects Heights, IL: Waveland Press.

Massey, D.S. (2007). *Categorically unequal: The American stratification system.* New York, NY: Russell Sage Foundation.

Matthews, R. (2009). 'Beyond "so what?" criminology: Rediscovering realism.' *Theoretical Criminology, 13,* 341–362.

Matthews, R.A. (2003). 'Marxist criminology.' In M.D. Schwartz and S.E. Hatty (Eds), *Controversies in critical criminology* (pp. 1–14). Cincinnati, OH: Anderson Publishing.

Matthews, R.A. (2006). 'Ordinary business in Nazi Germany.' In R.J. Michalowski and R.C. Kramer (Eds), *State–corporate crime: Wrongdoing at the intersection of business and government* (pp. 116–133). New Brunswick, NJ: Rutgers University Press.

Matthews, R.A., and Kauzlarich, D. (2006). 'The crash of ValuJet flight 592.' In R.J. Michalowski and R.C. Kramer (Eds), *State–corporate crime: Wrongdoing at the intersection of business and government* (pp. 82–97). New Brunswick, NJ: Rutgers University Press.

Mauer, M. (2005, October). 'Facts about prisoners and prisons.' *Sentencing Project*.

Melichar, K. (1990). 'Deconstruction: Critical theory or an ideology of despair.' *Humanity and Society, 12*, 366–385.

Merton, R.K. (1938). 'Social structure and anomie.' *American Sociological Review, 3*, 672–682.

Merz-Perez, L., and Heide, K.M. (2004). *Animal cruelty: Pathway to violence against people*. Lanham, MD: AltaMira Press.

Messerschmidt, J.W. (1993). *Masculinities and crime: Critique and reconceptualization*. Lanham, MD: Roman and Littlefield.

Messerschmidt, J.W. (1997). *Crime as structured action: Gender, race, class, and crime in the making*. Thousand Oaks, CA: Sage.

Messerschmidt, J.W. (2000). *Nine lives: Adolescent masculinities, the body, and violence*. Boulder, CO: Westview.

Messerschmidt, J.W. (2004). *Flesh and blood: Adolescent gender diversity and violence*. Lanham, MD: Rowman and Littlefield.

Messerschmidt, J.W. (2005). 'Men, masculinities, and crime.' In M.S. Kimmel, J. Hearn, and R.W. Connell (Eds), *Handbook of studies on men and masculinities* (pp. 196–212). Thousand Oaks, CA: Sage.

Messner, S., and Rosenfeld, R. (2006). *Crime and the American dream*. Belmont, CA: Wadsworth.

Michalowski, R.J. (1983). 'Crime control in the 1980s: A progressive agenda.' *Crime and Social Justice*, Summer, 13–23.

Michalowski, R.J. (1985). *Order, law, and crime: An introduction to criminology*. New York, NY: Random House.

Michalowski, R.J. (1996). 'Critical criminology and the critique of domination: The story of an intellectual movement.' *Critical Criminology, 7*, 9–16.

Michalowski, R., and Dubisch, J. (2001). *Run for the wall: Remembering Vietnam on a motorcycle pilgrimage*. New Brunswick, NJ: Rutgers University Press.

Miliband, R. (1969). *The state in capitalist society: The analysis of the western system of power*. London: Quartet.

Miller, J. (2001). *One of the guys: Girls, gangs, and gender*. New York, NY: Oxford University Press.

Miller, J. (2002). 'The strengths and limits of "doing gender" for understanding street crime.' *Theoretical criminology, 6*, 433–460.

Miller, J. (2003). 'Feminist criminology.' In M.D. Schwartz and S.E. Hatty (Eds), *Controversies in critical criminology* (pp. 15–28). Cincinnati, OH: Anderson Publishing.

Miller, J. (2008). *Getting played: African American girls, urban inequality, and gendered violence.* New York, NY: New York University Press.

Miller, S.L. (1994). 'Expanding the boundaries: Toward a more inclusive and integrated study of intimate violence.' *Violence and Victims, 9,* 183–194.

Miller, S.L. (1999). *Gender and community policing: Walking the walk.* Boston, MA: Northeastern University Press.

Mobley, A. (2003). 'Convict criminology: The two-legged data dilemma.' In J.I. Ross and S.C. Richards (Eds), *Convict criminology* (pp. 209–226). Belmont, CA: Wadsworth.

Monsebraaten, L., and Daly, R. (2007, November 26). 'Canada's poverty capital.' *Toronto Star,* A1, A6–A7.

Moore, M. (2003). *Dude, where's my country?* New York, NY: Warner Books.

Morash, M. (2006). *Understanding gender, crime, and justice.* Thousand Oaks, CA: Sage.

Morgan, D.H.J. (1992). *Discovering men.* London: Routledge.

Morris, R. (1995). *Penal abolition: The practical choice.* Toronto, ON: Canadian Scholars' Press.

Mujica, A., and Ayala, A.I.U. (2008). 'Femicide in Morelos: An issue on public health.' Paper presented at the World Health Organization's 9th World Conference on Injury Prevention and Safety Promotion, Yucatan, Mexico, March 18.

Mullins, C.W. (2006). *Holding your square: Masculinities, streetlife and violence.* Portland, OR: Willan.

Mullins, C.W. (2009). ' "He would kill me with his penis": Genocidal rape in Rwanda as a state crime.' *Critical Criminology, 17,* 15–34.

Mullins, C.W., and Rothe, D. (2008). *Blood, power, and bedlam: Violations of international criminal law in post-colonial Africa.* New York, NY: Peter Lang.

Muzzatti, S.L. (2005). 'Bits of falling sky and global pandemics: Moral panic and Severe Acute Respiratory Syndrome (SARS).' *Illness, Crisis and Loss, 13,* 117–128.

Muzzatti, S.L. (2006). 'Cultural criminology: A decade and counting of criminological chaos.' In W.S. DeKeseredy and B. Perry (Eds), *Advancing critical criminology: Theory and application* (pp. 63–82). Lanham, MD: Lexington Books.

Newburn, T., and Stanko, E.A. (1994). 'Introduction: Men, masculinities and crime.' In T. Newburn and E.A. Stanko (Eds), *Just boys doing business? Men, masculinities and crime* (pp. 1–9). London: Routledge.

O'Brien, M. (2005). 'What is *cultural* about cultural criminology?' *British Journal of Criminology, 45,* 599–612.

Ogle, R.S., and Batton, C. (2009). 'Revisiting patriarchy: Its conceptualization and operationalization in criminology.' *Critical Criminology, 17,* 159–182.

Oliver, W. (2006). 'The streets: An alternative black male socialization institution.' *Journal of Black Studies, 36,* 918–937.

Olsson, P. (2003). *Legal ideals and normative realities: A case study of children's rights and child labor activity in Paraguay.* Lund: Lund University.

Owen, B. (2005). 'Afterword.' In J. Irwin, *The warehouse prison: Disposal of the new dangerous class* (pp. 261–289). Los Angeles, CA: Roxbury.

Pager, D. (2007). *Marked: Race, crime, and finding work in an era of mass incarceration.* Chicago, IL: University of Chicago Press.

Parker, L. (2007). 'United Nations publishes handbook on restorative justice.' *Restorative Justice Online.* Retrieved January 28, 2010, from www.restorativejusice.org/editions/2007/feb07/unhandbook.

Pateman, C. (1988). *The sexual contract.* London: Polity.

Payne, B.K., and Gainey, R.R. (2006). *Family violence and criminal justice: A life course approach* (2nd ed.). Cincinnati, OH: Anderson Publishing.

Pearce, F. (1976). *Crimes of the powerful: Marxism, crime and deviance.* London: Pluto Press.

Pearce, F. (1992). 'The contribution of "left realism" to the study of commercial crime.' In J. Lowman and B.D. MacLean (Eds), *Realist criminology: Crime control and policing in the 1990s* (pp. 313–335). Toronto, ON: University of Toronto Press.

Pepinsky, H. (2008). 'Empathy and restoration.' In D. Sullivan and L. Tift (Eds), *Handbook of restorative justice* (pp. 188–197). London: Routledge.

Pepinsky, H., and Quinney, R. (Eds). (1991). *Criminology as peacemaking.* Bloomington, IN: Indiana University Press.

Perkins, D. (2010, January 22). 'Justice system key to ending hockey violence.' *Toronto Star,* S4.

Perry, B. (2003). 'Accounting for hate crime.' In M.D. Schwartz and S.E. Hatty (Eds), *Controversies in critical criminology* (pp. 147–160). Cincinnati, OH: Anderson Publishing.

Perry, B. (2006). 'Missing pieces: The paucity of hate crime scholarship.' In W.S. DeKeseredy and B. Perry (Eds), *Advancing critical criminology: Theory and application* (pp. 155–178). Lanham, MD: Lexington Books.

Perry, B. (2009a). 'Racist violence against Native Americans.' In B. Perry (Ed.), *Hate crimes volume 3: The victims of hate crime* (pp. 1–18). Santa Barbara, CA: Praeger.

Perry, B. (2009b). *Policing race and place in Indian country: Over- and under-enforcement.* Lanham, MD: Lexington Books.

Pfohl, S. (1994). *Images of deviance and social control: A sociological history.* New York, NY: McGraw-Hill.

Pitts-Taylor, V. (2007). *Surgery junkies: Wellness and pathology in cosmetic culture.* New Brunswick, NJ: Rutgers University Press.

Platt, A.M. (1969). *The childsavers.* Chicago, IL: University of Chicago Press.

Polk, K. (2003). 'Masculinities, femininities and homicide: Competing explanations for male violence.' In M.D. Schwartz and S.E. Hatty (Eds), *Controversies in critical criminology* (pp. 133–146). Cincinnati, OH: Anderson Publishing.

Porter, A. (2005). 'Restorative justice takes the world stage at United Nations crime conference.' *Restorative Practices eForum*, June 14. Retrieved January 27, 2010, from www.realjustice.org/library/uncrimecongress.html.

Pratt, T. (2009). *Addicted to incarceration: Corrections policy and the politics of misinformation in the United States.* Thousand Oaks, CA: Sage.

Presdee, M. (2000). *Cultural criminology and the carnival of crime.* London: Routledge.

Proudfoot, S. (2009, July 23). ' "Honor killings" of females on rise in Canada: Expert.' *The Star Pheonix*, 1.

Ptacek, J. (2010a). 'Editor's Introduction.' In J. Ptacek (Ed.), *Restorative justice and violence against women* (pp. ix–xiii). New York, NY: Oxford University Press.

Ptacek, J. (2010b). 'Resisting co-optation: Three feminist challenges to antiviolence work.' In J. Ptacek (Ed.), *Restorative justice and violence against women* (pp. 5–36). New York, NY: Oxford University Press.

Ptacek, J. (Ed.). (2010c). *Restorative justice and violence against women.* New York, NY: Oxford University Press.

Quinney, R. (1974). *Critique of the legal order.* Boston, MA: Little, Brown.

Quinney, R. (1975). 'Crime control in capitalist society: A critical philosophy of legal order.' In I. Taylor, P. Walton, and J. Young (Eds), *Critical criminology* (pp. 181–202). London: Routledge and Kegan Paul.

Quinney, R. (1991). 'The way of peace: On crime, suffering and service.' In H. Pepinsky and R. Quinney (Eds), *Criminology as peacemaking* (pp. 3–13). Bloomington, IN: Indiana University Press.

Radelet, M.R. (2005). 'Foreword.' In S.F. Sharp, *Hidden victims: The effects of the death penalty on families of the accused* (pp. vii–x). New Brunswick, NJ: Rutgers University Press.

Raphael, J. (2009). 'The trapping effects of poverty and violence.' In E. Stark and E.S. Buzawa (Eds), *Violence against women in families and relationships, volume 1* (pp. 93–110). Santa Barbara, CA: Prager.

Ratner, R.S. (1985). 'Inside the liberal boot: The criminological enterprise in Canada.' In T. Fleming (Ed.), *The new criminologies in Canada: State, crime, and control* (pp. 13–26). Toronto, ON: Oxford University Press.

Rebovich, D., and Layne, J. (2000). *The national survey on white collar crime*. Morgantown, WV: National White Collar Crime Center.

Reiman, J., and Leighton, P. (2010). *The rich get richer and the poor get prison: Ideology, class, and criminal justice* (9th ed.). Boston, MA: Allyn and Bacon.

Renzetti, C.M. (1994). 'On dancing with a bear: Reflections on some of the current debates among domestic violence theorists.' *Violence and Victims, 9*, 195–200.

Renzetti, C.M. (1999). 'Editor's introduction.' *Violence Against Women, 5*, 1235–1237.

Renzetti, C.M., and Maier, S.L. (2002). 'Private crime in public housing: Fear of crime and violent victimization among women public housing residents.' *Women's Health and Urban Life, 1*, 46–65.

Rigakos, G.S. (2002). *The new parapolice: Risk markets and commodified social control*. Toronto, ON: University of Toronto Press.

Robyn, L. (2006). 'Violations of treaty rights.' In R.J. Michalowski and R.C. Kramer (Eds), *State–corporate crime: Wrongdoing at the intersection of business and government* (pp. 186–198). New Brunswick, NJ: Rutgers University Press.

Rock, P. (1992). 'Foreword: The criminology that came in from the cold.' In J. Lowman and B.D. MacLean (Eds), *Realist criminology: Crime control and policing in the 1990s* (pp. ix–xii). Toronto, ON: University of Toronto Press.

Rosenau, P.M. (1992). *Postmodernism and the social sciences: Insights, inroads and intrusions*. Princeton, NJ: Princeton University Press.

Ross, J.I., and Richards, S.C. (2003). 'Introduction: What is the new school of convict criminology?' In J.I. Ross and S.C. Richards (Eds), *Convict criminology* (pp. 1–14). Belmont, CA: Wadsworth.

Rothe, D. (2009). *The crime of all crimes: An introduction to state criminality*. Lanham, MD: Roman and Littlefield.

Rothe, D., and Friedrichs, D.O. (2006). 'The state of the criminology of state crime.' *Social Justice, 3*, 147–161.

Rothe, D., Kramer, R., and Mullins, C.W. (2009). 'Torture, impunity, and open legal spaces: Abu Ghraib and international controls.' *Contemporary Justice Review, 12*(1), 27–43.

Rothe, D., and Mullins, C.W. (2006). *Symbolic gestures and the generation of global social control: The International Criminal Court.* Lanham, MD: Lexington Books.

Rothe, D., Ross, J.I., Mullins, C.W., Friedrichs, D.O., Michalowski, R., Barak, G., Kauzlarich, D., and Kramer, R.C. (2009). 'That was then, this is now, what about tomorrow: Future directions in state crime studies.' *Critical Criminology, 17*, 3–14.

Rubin, P. (2000). *Abused women in family mediation: A Nova Scotia snapshot.* Halifax, NS: Transition House Association of Nova Scotia.

Russell, D.E.H. (1993). *Against pornography: The evidence of harm.* Berkeley, CA: Russell Publications.

Russell, S. (2002). 'The continuing relevance of Marxism to critical criminology.' *Critical Criminology, 11*, 93–112.

Sartre, J.P. (1964). *The words.* London: Penguin.

Savelsberg, J.J., King, R., and Cleveland, L. (2002). 'Politicized scholarship: Science on crime and the state.' *Social Problems, 49*, 327–348.

Schissel, B. (1997). *Blaming children: Youth crime, moral panics and the politics of hate.* Halifax, NS: Fernwood.

Schlosser, E. (1998). 'The prison–industrial complex.' *Atlantic Monthly*, December, p. 54.

Schmalleger, F., and Volk, R. (2005). *Canadian criminology today: Theories and applications* (2nd ed.). Toronto, ON: Pearson Prentice Hall.

Schulte-Bockholt, A. (2006). *The politics of organized crime and the organized crime of politics.* Lanham, MD: Lexington Books.

Schur, E.M. (1984). *Labeling women deviant: Gender, stigma, and social control.* Philadelphia, PA: Temple University Press.

Schwartz, M.D. (1989). 'Asking the right questions: Battered wives are not all passive.' *Sociological Viewpoints, 5*, 46–61.

Schwartz, M.D. (1991). 'The future of critical criminology.' In B.D. MacLean and D. Milovanovic (Eds), *New directions in critical criminology* (pp. 119–124). Vancouver, BC: Collective Press.

Schwartz, M.D., and DeKeseredy, W.S. (1993). 'The return of the "battered husband syndrome" through the typification of women as violent.' *Crime, Law and Social Change, 20*, 249–265.

Schwartz, M.D., and DeKeseredy, W.S. (1997). *Sexual assault on the college campus: The role of male peer support.* Thousand Oaks, CA: Sage.

Schwartz, M.D., and DeKeseredy, W.S. (2008). 'Interpersonal violence against women.' *Journal of Contemporary Criminal Justice, 24,* 178–185.

Schwartz, M.D., and Friedrichs, D.O. (1994). 'Postmodern thought and criminological discontent: New metaphors for understanding violence.' *Criminology, 32,* 221–246.

Schwartz, M.D., and Friedrichs, D.O. (2004). 'Postmodern thought and criminological discontent: New metaphors for understanding violence.' *Criminology, 32,* 221–246.

Schwartz, M.D., and Hatty, S.E. (2003). 'Introduction.' In M.D. Schwartz and S.E. Hatty (Eds), *Controversies in critical criminology* (pp. ix–xvii). Cincinnati, OH: Anderson Publishing.

Schwartz, M.D., and Pitts, V. (1995). 'Exploring a feminist routine activities approach to explaining sexual assault.' *Justice Quarterly, 12,* 9–31.

Schwendinger, H., and Schwendinger, J.R. (1975). 'Defenders of order or guardians of human rights?' In I. Taylor, P. Walton, and J. Young (Eds), *Critical criminology* (pp. 113–146). London: Routledge and Kegan Paul.

Schwendinger, H., Schwendinger, J.R., and Lynch, M.L. (2008). 'Critical criminology in the United States: The Berkeley School and theoretical trajectories.' In K. Carrington and R. Hogg (Eds), *Critical criminology: Issues, debates, challenges* (pp. 41–72). Portland, OR: Willan.

Selman, D., and Leighton, P. (2010). *Punishment for sale: Private prisons and big business.* Lanham, MD: Roman and Littlefield.

Selva, L., and Bohm, R. (1987). 'A critical examination of the informalism experiment in the administration of justice.' *Crime and Social Justice, 29,* 43–57.

Service Canada. (2009). *Employment insurance (EI).* Retrieved September 30, 2009, from www.servicecanada.gc.ca/eng/ei/menu/eihome.shtml.

Sev'er, A. (2002). *Fleeing the house of horrors: Women who have left abusive partners.* Toronto, ON: University of Toronto Press.

Sev'er, A. (2008). 'Discarded daughters: The patriarchal grip, dowry deaths, sex ratio imbalances and foeticide in India.' *Women's Health and Urban Life, 7,* 56–75.

Sharp, S.F. (2005). *Hidden victims: The effects of the death penalty on families of the accused.* New Brunswick, NJ: Rutgers University Press.

Sherrill, R. (2001, January 8). 'Death trip: The American way of execution.' *Nation.* Retrieved January 25, 2010, from www.thenation.com/doc/20010108/sherrill.

Silvestri, M., and Crowther-Dowey, C. (2008). *Gender and crime.* London: Sage.

Simpson *v.* University of Colorado, Boulder, 500 F.3d 1170 (10 Cir. 2007).

Sinclair, R.L. (2002). *Male peer support and male-to-female dating abuse committed by socially displaced male youth: An exploratory study.* Doctoral dissertation. Ottawa, ON: Carleton University.

Skolnick, J. (1966). *Justice without trial.* New York, NY: Wiley and Sons.

Smandych, R. (1985). 'Marxism and the creation of law: Re-examining the origins of Canadian anti-combines legislation, 1890–1910.' In T. Fleming (Ed.), *The new criminologies in Canada: State, crime, and control* (pp. 87–99). Toronto, ON: Oxford University Press.

Smith, A. (2010). 'Beyond restorative justice: Radical organizing against violence.' J. Ptacek (Ed.), *Restorative justice and violence against women* (pp. 255–278). New York, NY: Oxford University Press.

Smith, M.D. (1983). *Violence and sport.* Toronto, ON: Butterworths.

Smith, M.D. (1990). 'Patriarchal ideology and wife beating: A test of a feminist hypothesis.' *Violence and Victims, 5,* 257–273.

Southern Poverty Law Center. (2003). *10 ways to fight hate on campus: A response guide for college activists.* Montgomery, AL: Author.

Sparks, R.F. (1980). 'A critique of Marxist criminology.' In N. Morris and M. Tonry (Eds), *Crime and justice: An annual review, volume 2* (pp. 159–210). Chicago, IL: University of Chicago Press.

Spitzer, S. (1975). 'Toward a Marxian theory of deviance.' *Social Problems, 22,* 638–651.

Stark, E. (2007). *Coercive control: How men entrap women in personal life.* New York, NY: Oxford University Press.

Statistics Canada. (2007a). *A comparison of urban and rural crime rates.* Ottawa, ON: Author.

Statistics Canada. (2007b, November 21). 'Adult and youth correctional services: Key indicators.' *The Daily,* 1–6.

Statistics Canada. (2009). 'Homicide in Canada.' *The Daily.* Retrieved January 6, 2010, from www.statcan.gc.ca/daily-quotidien/091028/dq091208a-eng.htm.

Steffensmeier, D., and Streifel, C. (1992). 'Time series analysis of the female percentage of arrests for property crimes, 1960–1985: A test of alternative explanations.' *Justice Quarterly, 9,* 77–104.

Strawson, J. (2003). 'Holy war in the media: Images of Jihad.' In S. Chermak, F.Y. Bailey, and M. Brown (Eds), *Media representations of September 11* (pp. 17–28). Westport, CT: Praeger.

Stubbs, J. (2008). 'Critical criminological research.' In T. Anthony and C. Cunneen (Eds), *The critical criminology companion* (pp. 6–17). Annandale, NSW: Hawkins Press.

Taylor, I. (1992). 'Left realist criminology and the free market experiment in Britain.' In J. Young and R. Matthews (Eds), *Rethinking criminology: The realist debate* (pp. 95–122). London: Sage.

Taylor, I., Walton, P., and Young, J. (1973). *The new criminology: For a social theory of deviance.* London: Routledge and Kegan Paul.

Tepperman, L. (2010). *Deviance, crime, and control* (2nd ed.). Toronto, ON: Oxford University Press.

Terrill, R.J. (2007). *World criminal justice systems.* Cincinnati, OH: LexisNexis.

Thomas, J., and O'Maolchatha, A. (1989). 'Reassessing the critical metaphor: An opportunistic revisionist view.' *Justice Quarterly, 2,* 143–172.

Toby, J. (1957). 'Social disorganization and stake in conformity: Complementary factors in the predatory behavior of young hoodlums.' *Journal of Criminal Law, Criminology and Police Science, 48,* 12–17.

Tombs, S., and Whyte, D. (2007). *Safety crimes.* Portland, OR: Willan.

Travers, J. (2007, October 23). 'On crime issue, facts don't matter.' *Toronto Star,* A18.

Travis, J., and Waul, M. (2003). 'Prisoners once removed: The children and families of prisoners.' In J. Travis and M. Waul (Eds), *Prisoners once removed: The impact of incarceration and reentry on children, families, and communities* (pp. 1–32). Washington, DC: Urban Institute Press.

Turpin-Petrosino, C. (2009). 'Black victimization: Perceptions and realities.' In B. Perry (Ed.), *Hate crimes volume 3: The victims of hate crime* (pp. 19–44). Santa Barbara, CA: Praeger.

United States Department of Labor. (2009). 'Title IX, education amendments of 1972.' Retrieved September 15, 2009, from www.dol.gov/oasam/regs/statutes/titleIX.htm.

United Way of Greater Toronto. (2007). *Losing ground: The persistent growth of family poverty in Canada's largest city.* Toronto, ON: Author.

Unnever, J.D., Cullen, F.T., Mathers, S.A., McClure, T.E., and Allison, M.C. (2009). 'Racial discrimination and Hirschi's criminological classic: A chapter in the sociology of knowledge.' *Justice Quarterly, 26,* 377–409.

Ursel, E. (1986). 'The state and maintenance of patriarchy: A case study of family and welfare legislation.' In J. Dickinsin and B. Russell (Eds), *Family, economy and state* (pp. 150–191). Toronto, ON: Garamond.

Van Dijk, J. (2008). *The world of crime: Breaking the silence on problems of security, justice, and development across the world*. Los Angeles, CA: Sage.

Van Dyke, N., and Tester, G. (2008). 'The college campus as defended territory: Factors influencing variation in racist hate crime.' Department of Sociology, Washington State University.

Van Ness, D. (2002). 'UN economic and social council endorses basic principles on restorative justice.' *Restorative Justice Online*. Retrieved January 28, 2010, from www.restorativejustice.org/editions/2002/August02/ECOSOC%20Acts.

Vogel, M.E. (2007). 'The irony of imprisonment: The punitive paradox of the carceral turn and the "micro-death" of the material.' In M. Vogel (Ed.), *Crime, inequality and the state* (pp. 1–50). London: Routledge.

Vold, G.B., Bernard, T.J., and Snipes, J.B. (2002). *Theoretical criminology* (5th ed.). New York, NY: Oxford University Press.

Wacquant, L. (2001). 'Deadly symbiosis: When ghetto and prison meet and mesh.' *Punishment and Society, 3*, 95–134.

Wacquant, L. (2008). *Urban outcasts: A comparative sociology of advanced marginality*. Malden, MA: Polity.

Wacquant, L. (2009). *Punishing the poor: The neoliberal government of social insecurity*. Durham, NC: Duke University Press.

Walker Rettberg, J. (2009). 'Joining a Facebook group as political action.' *jill/txt*. Retrieved January 20, 2010, from http://jilltxt.net/?p=2367.

Walklate, S. (1989). *Victimology*. London: Unwin Hyman.

Walklate, S. (2004). *Gender, crime and criminal justice* (2nd ed.). Devon: Willan.

Walters, R. (2003). 'New modes of governance and the commodification of criminological knowledge.' *Social and Legal Studies, 12*, 5–26.

Walther, J.B., Slovacek, C.L., and Tidwell, L.C. (2001). 'Is a picture worth a thousand words: Photographic images in long-term and short-term computer-mediated communication.' *Communication Research, 28*, 105–134.

Walton, P. (1998). 'Big science – dystopia and utopia – establishment and new criminology revisited.' In P. Walton and J. Young (Eds), *The new criminology revisited* (pp. 1–13). London: St. Martin's Press.

Walton, P., and Young, J. (1998). 'Preface.' In P. Walton and J. Young (Eds), *The new criminology revisited* (pp. vii–viii). London: St. Martin's Press.

Warr, M. (2002). *Companions in crime: The social aspects of criminal conduct*. New York, NY: Cambridge University Press.

Watts, C., and Zimmerman, C. (2002, April 6). 'Violence against women: Global scope and magnitude.' *The Lancet*, p. 359.

Websdale, N. (1998). *Rural woman battering and the justice system: An ethnography*. Thousand Oaks, CA: Sage.

Weitzer, R., and Kubrin, C.E. (2009). 'Misogyny in rap music: A content analysis of prevalence and meanings.' *Men and Masculinities, 12*, 3–29.

Werbowski, M. (2010, January 18). 'Prorogation nation in crisis: Is Canada sliding towards dictatorial rule?' *OhmyNews*, Retrieved January 20, 2010, from http://english.ohmynews.com/articleview/article_print.asp?menu=c10400andno=385899andr.

West, C. (2001). *Race matters*. New York, NY: Vintage.

West, C., and Zimmerman, D.H. (1987). 'Doing gender.' *Gender and Society, 1*, 125–151.

Western, B., Pattillo, M., and Weiman, D. (2004). 'Introduction.' In M. Pattillo, D. Weiman, and B. Western (Eds), *Imprisoning America: The social effects of mass incarceration* (pp. 1–18). New York, NY: Russell Sage Foundation.

Wheeler, S. (1976). 'Trends and problems in the sociological study of crime.' *Social Problems, 23*, 525–534.

Whittington, L. (2009a, September 10). 'Easing rules for EI "irresponsible": Liberal proposal to let more jobless quality would be ineffective and too expensive, Finley charges.' *Toronto Star*, A6.

Whittington, L. (2009b, July 7). 'Harper got it all wrong, budget watchdog says.' *Toronto Star*, A1.

Whittington, L., and Campion-Smith, B. (2010, January 20). 'PM makes Day chief cost-cutter.' *Toronto Star*, A6.

Willis, P. (1977). *Learning to labor: How working class kids get working class jobs*. New York, NY: Columbia University Press.

Wilson, J.Q. (1985). *Thinking about crime*. New York, NY: Vintage.

Wilson, W.J. (1987). *The truly disadvantaged: The inner-city, the underclass and public policy*. Chicago, IL: University of Chicago Press.

Wilson, W.J. (1996). *When work disappears: The world of the new urban poor*. New York, NY: Knopf.

Wilson, W.J., and Taub, R.P. (2008). *There goes the neighborhood: Racial, ethnic, and class tensions in four Chicago neighborhoods and their meaning for America*. New York, NY: Knopf.

Wonders, N.A. (1999). 'Postmodern feminist criminology and social justice.' In B.A. Arrigo (Ed.), *Social justice, criminal justice* (pp. 109–128). Belmont, CA: Wadsworth.

Young, J. (1971). *The drugtakers*. London: Paladin.

Young, J. (1988). 'Radical criminology in Britain: The emergence of a competing paradigm.' *British Journal of Criminology, 28,* 159–183.

Young, J. (1992). 'Ten points of realism.' In J. Young and R. Matthews (Eds), *Rethinking criminology: The realist debate* (pp. 24–68). London: Sage.

Young, J. (1998). 'Breaking windows: Situating the new criminology.' In P. Walton and J. Young (Eds), *The new criminology revisited* (pp. 14–46). London: St. Martin's Press.

Young, J. (1999). *The exclusive society.* London: Sage.

Young, J. (2004). 'Voodoo criminology and the numbers game.' In J. Ferrell, K. Hayward, W. Morrison, and M. Presdee (Eds), *Cultural criminology unleashed* (pp. 13–28). London: The Glasshouse Press.

Young, J. (2008). 'Critical criminology in the twenty-first century: Critique, irony and the always unfinished.' In K. Carrington and R. Hogg (Eds), *Critical criminology: Issues, debates, challenges* (pp. 251–274). Portland, OR: Willan.

Young, J. (2009, August 20). 'Mike Presdee: Perceptive sociologist who played a key role in the growth of cultural criminology.' *Guardian.* Retrieved December 3, 2009, from www.guardian.co.uk/education/2009/aug/20/obituary-mike-presdee/print.

Zerbisias, A. (2008, January 26). 'Packaging abuse of women as entertainment for adults: Cruel, degrading scenes "normalized" for generation brought up in dot-com world.' *Toronto Star,* L3.

Zorza, J. (2002). Domestic violence in rural America. In J. Zorza (Ed.), *Violence against women: Law, prevention, protection, enforcement, treatment, and health* (pp. 41-1 to 14-2). Kingston, NJ: Civic Research Institute.

INDEX